SOJOURN IN THE LAND OF
THE SIMMER DIM

SOJOURN IN THE LAND OF THE SIMMER DIM

by

D.B. SMITH

The Shetland Times Ltd.,
Lerwick, Shetland
1994

ISBN 0 900662 97 2
First published 1994

British Library Cataloguing-in-Publication Data
A catalogue record for this book is available from the British Library.

Front Cover: Hamnavoe, Burra Isle, Shetland, in the 1960s.
Photo: © Dennis Coutts

Printed and published by The Shetland Times Ltd., Prince Alfred Street, Lerwick, Shetland ZE1 0EP.
1994

CONTENTS

FOREWORD

Donald B. Smith's arrival in Shetland in 1966 as Principal Teacher of Modern Languages at the Anderson Institute saw the beginning of a love affair with the islands and its folk. The opening sentences of his account of that affair convey something of the deep, instinctive pull Shetland had for him and his family: *IT ALL BEGAN..........Was there really a beginning? Was it something inherited? Something I had no real control over? For, in a sense, the decision wasn't entirely mine!*

I can recall D.B.'s arrival at the school - the breezy personality alive with energy, the instant friendliness, the local lack of pretension. He rapidly found himself at home with staff and pupils.

The book is typical of the man. Memories tumble out as he relives those crowded years. His period at the Anderson Institute is described as "idyllic", its 400 pupils and 26 staff working in an intimate, family atmosphere, with co-operation and understanding.

Outside the school he felt equally at home and rapidly became involved in the local scene. His geniality and his genuine interest in people drew him into many friendships. He and his family established a special relationship with the Morrison family at their remote croft overlooking Swining Voe, which is fondly recorded in these pages. Among many evocations of Shetland life, he describes a trip to the herring fishing, two country weddings and Up-Helly-A'.

This little book is a testament of affection for the community which so obviously gave D.B. Smith and his family great pleasure. It also conveys something of the warmth and vitality of the man himself.

John J. Graham
February 1994.

ACKNOWLEDGEMENTS

FIRST and foremost to Shirley Peruniak, mother-in-law to our eldest daughter, Merilyn, now living in Alberta, Canada.

Shirley joined a First Aid class in Ontario, run by an ex-Wren who had served in Lerwick in the Navy during the War. She was quite amazed to meet someone in that area of Canada who knew of Shetland.

Shirley was curious to know how we came to live up in Shetland. This little book answers her question.

To Bill Rhind, the Headmaster of the Anderson Educational Institute, who answered my questions about the vacant post.

To the then Director of Education, John H. Spence, who appointed me.

To my colleagues in the AEI who accepted me.

To Drew Robertson, the late Bobby Burgoyne and the late Frank Sinclair and the other members of the Lerwick Brass Band.

To the Burra folk, especially the late Joe Laurenson, his widow Rachel, and their family and kith and kin of the *Venture*.

To Ron Caird, Syndication Dept. of D. C. Thomson & Co. Ltd., Dundee, who allowed us to print from the *People's Journal* (Northern), 'The Breekless Band'!

To John Graham, who so graciously offered to write the Foreword.

To my wife, Tib, who wholeheartedly backed me in the move into the unknown.

And particularly to those kindly old friends of Sandwick, Swining, with whom we treasure so many happy memories.

LIST OF ILLUSTRATIONS

1. Mr. & Mrs. Smith outside 82 King Harald Street

2. Jessie Irvine

3. Hilary and Merilyn Shetland-bound

4. First exchange group in Vosges

5. AEI staff 1966-67

6. AEI 6th year 1966-67

7. Long weekend at Olnafirth

8. Swining Voe

9. The *Venture*

10. Aboard a Soviet trawler

11. Joe Laurenson returns family and friends to Quarff

12. On board the *Agile*

13. The 1969 school party at Dundee station

14. Visiting friends

15. Article by D.B. Smith in the *Scottish Educational Journal* issue dated 12th September, 1969

MAKING THE DECISION

IT ALL BEGAN ... Was there really a beginning? Something I had no real control over? For, in a sense, the decision wasn't entirely mine!

In the autumn of 1965 I had been a candidate on a short leet for a post as assistant director of education in Orkney. At the interview, I calculated I'd spent one third of my time being taught, a third teaching others and I fancied spending the final third in administration. I didn't get the post.

However, it had been the most civilised interview I had had to date. I was seated at the open end of a square table; my audience on the other three sides were most attentive. What a contrast with my very first interview in Dundee City Chambers for a promoted post! In the vastness of the hall, a rammy of officials sat, yattering among themselves. Some must have been leaving the main business to the officials who had the qualifications to assess the candidates. One city father was busy filling in his football coupon for the week!

A couple of weeks after my trip to Kirkwall, during the Christmas holidays, a former colleague of Morgan Academy, Dundee, rang to ask me if I was interested in the vacant post of Head of the Modern Languages department in the Anderson Educational Institute in Lerwick.

"Anna, I wouldn't be seen dead in the place!"

In the summer of 1958, we had been invited by a sister-in-law to take the opportunity of visiting her and her family in Shetland before they left to return to the mainland of Scotland. Our young families got on well together. We four grown-ups had kept in contact happily. It would be a relatively cheap holiday and certainly an adventure.

We took the best route, sailing on board the *St Clair*, from Aberdeen at 6pm, due to dock in the heart of Lerwick at 8am next morning. Our little daughters, Merilyn aged six years and Hilary two and a half years, had an exciting time exploring the ship before we sailed. A great novelty was to sleep in bunks with a port-hole by their heads.

A fellow-passenger engaged my wife in conversation. She was returning to her home in Gulberwick. Tib has kept in touch with Jessie Irvine ever since. She no longer lives in the hamlet. Old age caught up with her. Like Big Baba, the great-great-gran of our Canadian grandchildren, in her 97th year, she lives in an Old Folk's Home, closer to her many aquaintances and friends in Lerwick.

It was a good holiday. Surprisingly, in the three weeks we stayed, it hardly rained at all. We had four dull days. For the rest of the time, the sun shone from about 2am till almost midnight. We had our own beach 50 yards from the house. The house itself was on a side road with little traffic and no obvious neighbours.

Five bairns were free to play in a fair-sized garden. We had no fears of them getting run over by vehicles, since the gate to the road was not easily opened.

As a holiday spot, in our circumstances, it was ideal. But we were a good 25 miles out of the metropolis, Lerwick. The house was surrounded by a wilderness of wind-swept moor, pock-marked with tiny Shetland sheep and scarred with peat-banks, where the drying peats were awaiting transport to the shed. There wasn't a tree in sight, but eastwards, hundreds of square miles of vibrant North Sea away beyond the beach, swished gentle onto the shingle or roared against the rocks.

A rare trip for provisions into Lerwick did little to enamour me of the town.

"No, Anna, I wouldn't be seen dead in the place!"

After the Christmas festivities in our home in Dundee, I took a trip south to Teesside to visit my folks. I spoke of the Shetland post. My parents, then verging on their '70s, did not suggest that I should forget about it. Two hundred and fifty miles already separated us. Going north to Lerwick would double that separation.

Nothing was said either way. I had been away from my native heath for the past 25 years — university, South Africa with the RAF in the war, France in training for my career and Dundee in the Morgan for a good 18 years.

I returned north.

It was Hogmanay. The bells had rung in the New Year. We could hear voices at the front door! A young ex-colleague, his wife and a couple of friends were outside to 'first-foot' us. In they came.

There was quite a bit of catching-up to do. George had seized the opportunity of an early promotion by accepting the post of Head of Department (Modern Languages) in the High School in Kingussie.

He spoke of it enthusiastically. "It's fantastic! I am running my own department. The village is in the Highlands on the main A9 route from Inverness to the south. It's a hive of activity. I play the fiddle. Ceilidhs, the local gatherings with their music, dancing and conversation, are delightfully hospitable."

His wife, being a trained doctor, was doing an important job as a locum and, in off-duty hours, could satisfy her interest in drama. Financially, he was only £120 per annum better off. That sum was the level of the responsibility payment for his post in a small secondary school.

His enthusiasm gave me food for thought. Lerwick had more to offer as a financial inducement for, as well as the responsibility element, there was an extra payment for 'remote living'. (For service on one of the many islands off the Shetland Mainland, there was a further addition for more remoteness!)

It must have been a fortnight or so later. I picked up the phone.

"Anna, if I was interested in the Shetland job, who would I get in touch with?"

"Give the headmaster a ring."

It was a Thursday evening in early January. I dialled. I was speaking to the headmaster.

"Ah! The appointment to the post for head of the Modern Languages Department is being decided tomorrow. Can you give me details of your qualifications?"

I did, and added, "If the post is not filled, please could you let me know tomorrow evening after 6? We have to pick up our daughters from their dancing-class. It won't be until after 6 before we are home."

That Friday evening, another voice spoke. It was the Director of Education for Shetland.

"Mr Smith? Would I be able to meet you in Dundee on Wednesday. The gentleman who was interviewed for the post, did not accept it. I shall be coming in the train from Aberdeen en route to a meeting in Glasgow."

"Certainly. I shall pick you up at Tay Bridge Station." That was that.

(Most likely the interviewee had had a difficult decision to make. On the one hand, there was promotion, on the other, he probably felt his allegiance lay with his senior pupils in his own school. They were now in the final term before their Higher Certificate exams. A replacement for him would not be found right away: advertising for his vacant post, the drawing up of the leet, interviewing and then, the month of notice to be given by his successor, would all add to the delay.)

On that Wednesday, I met John H. Spence and drove him up to our house in my car. He interviewed me on my own lounge carpet! I had discussed the matter with my better half.

"If he offers me the job, shall I take it? We'll be jumping into the middle of the North Sea. If you don't fancy the idea, I'm not accepting."

"No, we'll go."

She was getting more concerned about the lunch. The veg was cooling off, if we didn't come to a decision!

That was it. John H. offered me the job. I accepted. I was to take up post as from 12th February, 1966.

The interview had taken place on Wednesday, 12th January. The regulations demanded that I give a month's notice to my employing authority, hence the commencing date in Shetland, 12th February. It was a Saturday. The first boat north had to be the Monday boat on the propitious date of St Valentine's Day, 14th February! Might this date forge the first link in a romantic chain, binding us to the islands and the Shetland folk?

ARRIVAL AT 82, KING HARALD STREET

IN DUNDEE, we owned our own house. The Shetland authority was offering us the lease of a house. This policy influenced prospective teachers into taking the plunge and cutting ties they might have with mainland Britain.

Only recently, we had moved into a new house and carried out some decorating. Shetland offered to do up their house. My wife felt she would like to be on hand to have some say in colour schemes and choice of wallpapers. This was agreed.

Our problem now was to accommodate our three daughters. Merilyn was into her 2nd year at Morgan. Deirdre, the youngest, was in her 2nd year at school. Hilary needed two and a half years to complete primary. We decided to give the younger girls a short winter break with us for one week. Kind neighbours took Merilyn in with their family.

Since we had a car, we felt it would be a good idea to load it as much as possible with small items, leaving the main 'flitting' to the experts later on.

Mid-February is still winter with us. In fact, there had been a fall of snow earlier in the week before our sailing. Among the items we took was a spade, in case we had to dig ourselves out on the road to Aberdeen! On the roof-rack, wrapped in a large plastic sheet, was a mattress. In the new house, I would have to make that my bed down on the floor. For the week of their stay, the girls had camp-beds.

The coast road up to Aberdeen rises quite high above the sea. At Catterline we stopped for petrol. It seemed that the spade was going to come in useful. There was a coating of snow all around. However, it was nothing more than that. The road trip was uneventful.

I was to sail on quite a few occasions between Aberdeen and Shetland; so, my memory of this trip is unclear.

Next morning, the *St Clair* tied up at her berth right in the centre of the harbour frontage. The grey town rises steeply up to the ridge of Hillhead. Across the water lies Bressay. At its southern end, this island rises to the elegant summit of The Ward. Snow-speckled, it brought to mind the shapely cone of the Japanese holy mountain of Fujiyama.

We were directed to the Education Offices. Naturally, I had to report there to let them know of my presence, but equally importantly, I needed to receive the keys to No. 82 King Harald Street, our future home.

No. 82 was last but one in a terrace. At the end of King Harald Street which sloped down to the north, we caught a glimpse of the sea. The houses were three storeys high. The street was wide, flanked on the other side by similar houses which towered higher, as they were built on ground rising to another ridge. We were to learn that these residences and ours had been the homes of the herring barons, who had made their fortunes from the 'silver darlings'. The seas round Shetland abounded in fish.

For bairns, a new house is a source of excitement. Hilary and Deirdre wasted no time in exploring. The bare stairway echoed with the clatter of their feet, as they dashed up the stairs. On the top floor, they came upon three small bedrooms, just right, one for each of our girls.

More sedately, but perhaps no less excitedly, Tib and I checked out the lower part of the house. There was a front room at street level. Beyond, to the back was the kitchen where an Aga cooker would burn. Further to the back was the scullery. A door from it opened into the garden.

We returned to the hallway. The stair led up in line with the front door to a mid-landing. A frosted-glass door opened into a draughty big bathroom with a high ceiling. I feel the shivers now, as I think of it!

From the mid-landing a short stair led back to the main landing. Off it, was another front room, spacious and high-ceilinged and a small room I could claim as a study which overlooked the street. A third room, above the kitchen and having the main chimney flue built into its north wall, was to be our bedroom. The house had no central heating. That was not a general feature in houses in the 1960s. We had little need of it. The Aga gave out so much heat downstairs, that we should have stifled in the kitchen with the door shut. Keeping the door open allowed heat to rise up the stairwell and take the chill off the house. The chimney flue, passing up from the Aga warmed the wall at the head of our bed.

This was the residence which the authority had agreed to repaint and decorate. In the week she was there, Tib chose the wallpaper and paint for the various rooms and gave instructions to the painters who were allotted to the job.

That first week, whatever it held for me, was quite a traumatic experience for my family. The change of climate, colder, damper, a wind that never stopped blowing, gentle or stormy, had its effect on Hilary. She caught a chill. The cold, empty house did not help matters.

Arrangements for the re-decoration led to discussions, changes of plans, suggestions, consultations, decisions in shops with decorators and house-furnishers, until Tib was satisfied her requirements would be met. The week ended in a final upset.

It was felt that Hilary was so unwell, it would be better to get back to Dundee as soon as possible. They would take the plane, another thrill for the bairns and their mum!

When they arrived over Dyce, the airport for Aberdeen, fog was so thick, the plane could not land. It was redirected to Turnhouse, the Edinburgh airport. BEA as it then was, arranged for a bus service to transport the passengers to their home areas. Our little group arrived in Perth. There they had to find their own way home on the local bus to Dundee. Finally, they had to trudge in deep snow from the bus to the house.

At No. 82, I had to find a modus vivendi. Matters were simplified as far as bed and board went. The mattress on the floor was quite comfortable. The only thing was that I had to move it from time to time, as the decorators moved into what had been my bedroom to get on with its decoration. They were an amiable bunch of lads, glad, no doubt that they had indoor work to do at that time of the year.

Breakfast was no problem, nor was lunch. The school had a canteen for pupils and staff. Food was well prepared, varied and served in satisfying portions. My new colleagues and their wives took pity on me in my solitude. I was invited out to supper.

INTRODUCING THE AEI

THE SCHOOL needed me urgently. Senior pupils were only a couple of months away from their Higher Certificate exams. In the Scottish system, good Highers offered the qualifications necessary for entrance to university courses. I was the only member of staff fully qualified to teach modern languages.

My assistant was Adelaide Manson, who had long experience of primary school education. During her university career, she had gained a qualification in French, but had not had the need to use it. (By the end of the 1960s, this was to change. Primary schools were to adopt new theories, boosted by the 'Leeds Experiment', where, in unusual circumstances, a P7 class had had as its teacher a lady from Alsace, who, in the post-scholarship weeks of the summer term, thought it was a good idea to bring French into the classroom. The novelty was highly successful!)

We had two colleagues, a young Frenchman, acting as the 'assistant français', and a young lady who had worked abroad in a secretarial capacity. Her French was very fluent but slightly lacked the grammatical background which counted so importantly in the assessment of a candidate's ability at the final exams.

The Anderson Educational Institute had been built on the east-facing slope of the Knab, a promontory which gave an extensive view of the 'sooth mooth', the roadstead between Bressay and the mainland. We, having come from Aberdeen, were known as 'sooth-moothers'.

With the passage of time, it had become necessary to extend the original school with a modern building. This now incorporated the admin block and headmaster's office, an assembly hall and stage, gymnasium, staffroom, music-room, and science and technical block. The hall was decorated with a frieze, depicting the history of the islands from the earth dwellings of Jarlshof to modern times. The pupils of the school had created this most artistic piece.

The language department was based in the old school. I occupied a room on the upper floor. A stair led to Miss Manson's room below. Next door to my room, a storeroom held our supplies of textbooks and jotters. One day, as I was checking over a box, I discovered it contained a stock, in pristine condition, of a fairy-story book, that I had first become familiar with thirty-three years before.

I opened it. There before my eyes, the story began: 'Il y avait une fois trois ours ...!' Goldilocks!

There are fewer and fewer of us now, who first read the fairy-tale of our childhood in that book in French; and, I am sure, many of us can still repeat those opening words. They are a password back to many, many shared memories.

From my windows I looked down on the sound between Bressay and Lerwick. This made me only too readily aware of the movement of all manner of craft sailing past below the school — the *Clair*, fishing-boats, the Bressay ferry, Soviet trawlers and their water-tanker, the *Kandagatch*. She came in regularly to take on water for the fishing-fleet and processing factory-ship, which was operating out in the sea to our east.

So much that was new was going on about me that I came to school with my camera slung about my neck. For the first week, at least, I would dart to the window and snap some marine activity, particularly the fishing-boats as they returned, accompanied by the ever-present retinue of raucous screeching gulls.

From this classroom vantage point, the Ward looked even more like Fuji. At its summit stood the TV mast which let Lerwegians tune in to BBC1, the only channel we could get, whilst mainland Scots had the choice of BBC2 and ITV's programmes.

The AEI was the main secondary school. Successful pupils could go on to university and technical college education on the Scottish mainland.

From the scattered archipelago which made up a total population of some 18,000 souls, youngsters of secondary school age were sent to the school. This meant that, even on the Mainland of Shetland, quite a number of scholars had to live the weekdays in town in private 'digs' or in the hostels built next to the school. Children from such inaccessible islands as Fair Isle, Foula or the Out Skerries, more or less said 'Goodbye' to family from the age of 11 or 12. They could only get home at the end of term, if, and sometimes it was a big IF, the ferry to the island could make it. Virtually, it meant that families had to accept the fact that children might easily leave the nest from early teens, only to return at vacation times or at an annual holiday period. Once they were settled furth of Shetland, those visits would be rarer. This was one of the facts we would have to consider later in educating our own girls.

When I look back over the period of my stay at the AEI, I consider it was idyllic. The school population was about 400 pupils, boys and girls, taught by a staff of some 30 men and women. Most of these were former pupils of the school. In that respect, they had a better understanding of their pupils' background than the rest of us 'incomers'. It did not necessarily lead to a narrowness of outlook, a kind of educational inbreeding.

Shetlanders are great travellers. In some remote croft, one may easily stumble across the man of the house who can speak two or three foreign languages. It was reported that a Soviet sailor who jumped ship to escape the Communist régime found himself knocking at the door of a croft, to be answered in Russian by the far-travelled crofter. At this early point in my career in Shetland, I wasn't to know just how useful my own knowledge of languages would be.

In the staffroom, a refreshingly new atmosphere confronted me. Morgan with over 1000 pupils, had a staff of eighty or more teachers. There were two separate staffrooms; ours, for the men, had been converted from a storeroom. The ceiling was so low, that the electric light bulbs over the table tennis were not immune from smash hits! The art and science teachers who reigned above, organised their own 'tea-break' circles, as did the 'techy' squad in the workshops on the ground floor. So, there was a significant lack of contact between fellow-teachers in our different disciplines. And once the 'smokers' got lit up in our staffroom, visual contact was considerably less, too!

The AEI staffroom was in the modern section of the school. It had wide windows looking out onto the driveway into the school.

We didn't need this viewpoint to be warned of the arrival of inspectors. All over Shetland, the movement of many minions of the Establishment, police, customs, tax men, you name them, was evident to the ferryman or the person responsible for the ship's manifest or the plane's passenger list. Next minute, on the island to be visited by authority, unlicensed cars disappeared off the roads, illicit manufactories would be dismantled and the names of the inspecting officials would pass from Sumburgh or the harbour office via the grapevine to the ears of those most interested.

All twenty-six of us, including our headmaster, shared the bright, airy staffroom. A screen, folding concertina-style, could be manoeuvred into place so that half of the room might be used as a prep or marking-room for staff members. I rarely remember it being pulled into place. Most of us had ample space in our own rooms where everything was to hand, so marking and prep were done there.

The head, Bill Rhind, had been head of the maths department before his advancement. Quite a few of his colleagues had been his pupils. This fact and the intimacy of the staffroom space allowed for a degree of informality I had not known so far in my career. Today, in schools, there is openness in discussion, but, often there has to be a special calling together of staff or recall before the end of the holidays for what is euphemistically termed in the jargon, 'In-service training'. In the AEI we could all discuss matters amicably over our coffee and biscuits at break-time.

A member of staff who shared the staffroom with us was a fairly recent appointee. George Black was our technician. Where teachers might wear gowns, George wore a lab coat.

One day, probably in the first term of the new session of 1969, in he came. Ulster had witnessed trouble breaking out. In matter-of-fact tones George uttered words that I am sure his listeners and millions of other folk since, would wish had never been said. "YOU'LL NEVER SEE THE END OF THIS!"

In her sexy, guttural voice, Marlene Dietrich used to sing a song, 'Where have all the flowers gone?' It ended in a despairing refrain ...

It has just struck me forcibly, that away back in that year, the old Ulster folk of that generation were to know, in their dying days, sudden bereavement in the deaths of their friends, neighbours, even of family, victims of a bomb exploding in a street or shopping mall.

In that same year, our contemporaries were facing similar tragedy, or even manufacturing the weapons of slaughter. The older ones of our children's age-group were toting guns and planting bombs.

Today, 25 years further on, still in Ulster, the older peers of our grand-children's generation are hooding themselves, stealing cars and motorbikes, to go off on raids. They knock on a door. An unsuspecting man goes to answer. He falls dying in a spray of bullets. At another target, they spray bullets indiscriminately at the wrong crowd in the wrong pub at the wrong time.

Do the youngsters of that same generation, armed with make-believe pistols and Kalashnikovs, play, not at 'Cowboys and Indians' or 'Cops and Robbers' as we did in our childhood, but at 'Provos and Prots', squirming, then lying still, pretending to be 'dead' knowing that in ten minutes, Mam will be calling them in for tea?

The haunting refrain of Marlene's song, comes back to mind, repeated: 'When will they ever learn? When will they ever learn?'

That for all these years I have never forgotten George's words, is proof of how dramatic was their effect.

The contrast to all this was found in the atmosphere of co-operation and understanding, illustrated away down the school in the 1st year. Little souls readily knocked on Bill's door as if he was their favourite uncle. And he saw to it that they found their class again.

The intimacy which ruled in the school came clearly home to me on my first Saturday in the town. It was an island intimacy. Every Shetlander walking about the place doing the weekly shopping knew every other Shetlander to a greater or lesser degree. Many were inter-related.

I could see my new pupils nudging a senior member of the family, grandparent, parent, uncle, aunt, brother, sister, friend or neighbour. I stuck out like the proverbial sore thumb, made more obvious by the additional dressing of a camera, borne American tourist-style, belly-button pendant.

"Grandpa, that's our new French teacher." Heads turned, eyes glanced, scrutinised, mental notes were made. I might grimace in a friendly sort of way. I was an incomer. One day I should have to prove myself.

The world assumed smaller dimensions. Willie Thomson, my colleague in geography, was the son of the lecturer in my training college days who had taken the classes in religious education.

Jim Coull, the head of the 'techy' department was the son of the Broughty Ferry lifeboat coxswain, one of whose daughters had married a Belgian comrade-in-arms who had got his wings with me in Vereeniging in South Africa in 1943!

The wife of the young science master, Garry Williamson, had been the lass, eight years earlier, with whom I had passed the time of day, as I pushed my bike up Dales Voe from Sullom Voe. She had been mowing the lawn on that Saturday afternoon, when, for the first time, I had risked going for a bike run after my confrontation with polio and its after effects, a weak left leg.

I was soon to learn that folk knew more about me than I realised. Walking down Harbour Street, I was hailed from across the road by a complete stranger.

"I hear you play the clarinet. How about joining the Brass Band?"

I crossed over to Jimmy Dorrat, quite puzzled that he should know of my interest in music. He didn't know, however, how much of a tiro I was. I had taken up the instrument four or five years earlier, when Merilyn was beginning to take piano lessons. I thought, "If she sees me doing my daily practice stint, she might be encouraged to do likewise on her piano." She was! But there were to be repercussions!

One piece of advice we were given early in our days in Shetland was to decide on a club or society to join. We were warned that if we did not make such a decision, we should find ourselves involved in a host of activities. It was even said that folk, in such a situation, had found Shetland life so hectic, they had 'upped-sticks' and headed back to the city, for the peace and quiet it offered in the anonymity one could find there!

I decided to give the Band a 'go'.

Teaching in the AEI had facets that one would rarely meet in major mainland schools. It had been my habit in the Morgan classroom to call boys by their surnames and the girls by their Christian names. Imagine, then, my surprise when, looking at John Tait, I called out 'Tait!' and another four boys stood up, all Taits! From that day on, all my pupils were known by their Christian names or even by-names. There could be more than one John or Willie Tait in the room. 'Peerie' Willie would distinguish him from the bigger youth of the same Tait name. 'Peerie' is 'wee' or 'little' in the Shetland tongue.

A senior class, 5th year, was taking Higher French. I began my question at the back corner of the room. No answer! I was looking at a head bowed to hide the shame of not knowing the answer. I went on to the next pupil. Another bowed head! Then another and another, until the whole class sat with heads bowed!

Yet, they were far from cowed. The 6th year girls had completed their year of study. Highers were over by early May. Almost two months lay ahead. This was the normal situation in the Scottish system. Most of the rest of the school would also have finished the routine year's work, term exams being held once the Highers were out of the way.

This led to a tendency to want to free-wheel. Events like school sports, both internal and inter-school, had to be carried out. Inter-house matches in cricket, netball and swimming were important. The music department would be called on to provide entertainment at the final Prize-giving day. All of this activity would disrupt classes, as individuals were asked to be excused to attend one of these social events in rehearsals.

On this particular occasion, the 6th year young ladies were feeling quite bolshie. Work had no appeal. There was not the same tendency in the Shetland summer for them to say 'May we go outside and take our books out into the sun?' Unless one could find a sheltered corner away from the perpetual breeze, the warmth of the sun had little effect. I rounded on them in an attempt to boss them into doing some work.

"The trouble with you lot is, we've got to sugar the pill for you."

For a split second, there was dead silence. Then, a great hoot of laughter! This was one of those moments when one realises that the old words have lost their meaning and are clothed in another. THE PILL was just coming into its own as a contraceptive!

A livelier bunch was a 3rd year class of girls and boys. In these traditionally Scottish co-ed groups, the rivalry is intense. With a top section, it is 'all systems go'.

One occasion ought to have been memorable for quite a sentimental reason. It was St Valentine's Day, 1967. Just a year before, we had set out from Dundee on our Shetland adventure.

For one of the boys in the class, it was red-letter day, his 15th birthday. He shared it with his twin brother, who was in the other section with Miss Manson, one floor below.

The girls in the class were well aware of this event in the twin McRobbie boys' lives.

"Please, sir, it is Andrew and Raymond McRobbie's birthday today and we have a Valentine Card for them. Can we get them both together for the occasion?"

It could be that I needed to see the young gentleman on some matter concerning his studies; so, eagerly, one of the young ladies dashed downstairs to bring up the 'victim'.

He duly arrived, looking a bit woe-begone. 'What have I been up to now?'

might have been the question bothering him, as he stood in the presence of the head of the department.

I re-assured him. "It's all right, McRobbie. The young ladies have a surprise for you."

I called his twin out to join him.

"Happy Birthday!" the class chorused. "Here is your birthday card."

The artist amongst them (and they didn't lack for talent) handed over a large card which depicted a local Whalsay boat, bearing the twins across the sea, in which the 'sirens' swam, luring them on. 'Balloons' billowed from their smiling lips, verses of endearment, typical of the Valentine rhymes for the day.

I don't know whether the McRobbie boys still treasure that card or whether any of the poetesses remember the jingles. I have composed something of the flavour in:

> Hostel custard's always lumpy,
> Makes you feel a kinda jumpy.
> Jump overboard into the brine,
> And let our arms around you twine!

(Why I have recalled the hostel custard can only be because those pupils who had to live in the hostels had a poor opinion of the grub they got. School lunches, served in the school canteen, were top-notch.)

When I think back to those days in the AEI and recall pupils I taught, I find that many of them set up a partnership in marriage, like many of their predecessors. I have a feeling that Islands and, to some extent, Highland schools have a greater proportion of pupils who married school friends than might be the case elsewhere in the UK where the population is more mobile. I was told that, in general, a Shetland lass marrying south, would end up bringing her spouse back home to Shetland.

One young couple, who, by now, may have celebrated their Silver Wedding, used to drive about in a vehicle with a Borders registration. Those letters on a car's number-plate have been of interest to me from my own boyhood. We used to spend hours by the roadside in the 1930s logging number-plates. It had a practical application later in the war years. As a serviceman, hitch-hiking back home, I was in luck if a 'UP', 'PT', 'EF', 'XG' or a 'DC' pulled up. They were from my Teesside home district. That hardly applies today. Vehicles may have been registered there, but after a sale, may hardly ever be back 'home' again.

The Shetland vehicle I took special interest in bore the appropriate letters 'SH'! Whenever I meet the couple, I put my fingers to my lips, and whisper 'Sh!' I never clyped!

Because of certain long-established traditions, school life at the AEI was rich. As an outsider, I should attribute it to the islanders' need to entertain themselves. TV reception was not all that reliable and sets were not so advanced to give the clear pictures we know today.

I felt at home with them. Their way of life was close to what I had experienced in my childhood, when families made their own fun, round the piano or led by someone who played the fiddle, melodeon or mouth-organ.

Up-Helly-A', the fire festival, celebrated at the end of January, held a key to the artistic interests of the folk. There was the dressing-up. Why call the participants Guizers, unless that had something to do with it? Music is an integral part of the festival, as is the presentation of various sketches by the squads. Many skills of craftsmen and artists are demanded to make the festival the colourful, witty, lively event that it is.

A drama festival brings together competing teams from the communities of the islands. Tom Anderson and his Forty Fiddlers, the Lerwick Brass Band, the Choral Group, all added to the sum of talent.

Of all the school events, the Beanfeast, organised by the senior pupils as their party in the autumn term, epitomised these dramatic, artistic and musical skills. The first half was devoted to items not only of conventional musical entertainment, but also of parody, in which members of staff were the butt of the jests, taken in good part. A supper which lived up to the standard of the entertainment, filled the interval. Dancing followed, pupils and teachers mingling as partners. The belles of the ball did not lack for escorts, whether fellow-pupils or staff! The tasteful décor, supervised by the art department, was the handiwork of the seniors.

My own happy memories of my own schooldays tie up with extra-mural events, extra-mural in the sense of outside the walls of the classroom, and having little to do with class work. I have no doubt, that the young folk I knew in those years 1966-69, will have for ever, wonderful memories of the part they played in their presentation of *Peer Gynt* and *HMS Pinafore*. Certain performances were not only moving to the players but to their audience as well. Those who do not take part in school life like this are the losers.

Family ties and remoteness offered pupils a chance for lengthy breaks. To equal them, their mainland confrères would have had to resort to lengthy terms of truancy. A family wedding on the Out Skerries gave privileged school-age guests the occasion to enjoy a good week away from books.

The wind-swept outcrop of rock with a bare five miles of roadway on it, was only accessible by boat. That would be a local fishing-boat, not a timetabled ferry. The same boat would use its derricks and fish-hold to embark the liquid refreshment which a drouthy wedding-party would need to see them through the celebrations. Though a pupil might be advised against being absent for such a length of time, permission was rarely refused for him or her to attend.

Even a wedding celebration within reach of bus, taxi or car service, could be expected to last at least two, if not three days, in country districts.

On the first, the official ceremony would take place. By the time the traditional wedding-breakfast had been eaten and the dancing begun, they would be into the next day, and possibly, not into bed until daylight. After a spell of sleep there would still be the tidying-up to do, which might easily unite, if not the musicians of the previous evening, at least some equally talented folk whose playing would make the work lightsome and lead on into another evening of dance and song.

The evening and the morning were the third day!

MARCH WINDS AND APRIL SHOWERS!!!

THE ACCEPTANCE of the post in the AEI was a great adventure. What a contrast to the reception I had when I informed folk in Dundee of my decision.

"What's this I hear? You are taking up a post in Shetland? You've no idea of the weather they get up there, gales at any time of the year, rain and mist. You'll be wanting back in next to no time".

This was the sort of comment we faced from colleagues and family. Yet, our three-week holiday in 1958 was idyllic in contrast to these comments. Out of those 21 days, we had had only four of rain or mist. For the rest of the time, the sun had broken through cloud or had beamed down on us for the longest days of daylight we had ever known. They must have dawned at about 2 a.m. At the other end of the day, returning from a visit to Toft, we loitered up Dales Voe in a gloaming which began round about 11 p.m., just allowing the sun time to dip imperceptibly below the horizon.

More recently, on a return visit to Burra in 1985 (significantly similar digits!), I took a snap of Foula from Hamnavoe in the same gloaming and one next morning in sunlight, just to prove that it really was Foula on the evening shot!

Before I launch into the gales, a mistaken idea of the position of Shetland needs correcting. My 5th year class in Morgan Academy, kindly offered me, as a farewell token, a little handbook that they thought would be of help in my new surroundings. It's title was: GAELIC without GROANS!

I had to point out that Shetland had little to do with Gaeldom. It's ties were Norse. I settled for a Bartholomew's '1/2 inch' map of Shetland which was more useful, even to the completion of this book!

Sea travel was one essential problem we had to come to terms with, where meteorology plays a commanding role.

I am no sailor.

It was the Easter break. My first term in the Anderson Educational Institute was over. I had to head south without delay, back to Dundee to be on hand for the flitting. There, in reality, I was just a presence. During my term in Shetland, my wife had conducted the sale of our Dundee house and arranged for the transport to Lerwick of our goods and chattels through the services of the long-established Aberdeen firm, The Shore Porters.

It was the Thursday of the 1966 General Election which put Harold Wilson at the head of a Labour government. There must have been much rejoicing amongst my socialist colleagues of the AEI and the 'Parliament' which met in the shop in Brown's Buildings at the foot of King Harald Street under the chairmanship of the proprietor, Alex Morrison.

The election date I have not pin-pointed exactly, but the weather of the day has left an indelible impression.

I set off for the last day of term in my car. It stayed parked outside the door of No. 82; no fear of teenage tear-aways doing hand-brake turns in King Harald Street which could easily have accommodated their wild folly.

We had had a slight fall of snow. The evidence lay on the roof of the car. A thaw was setting in. The snow-melt trickled down the rear window onto the lid of the boot. It never reached the ground! An icy wind from the north froze it in its flow!

From my classroom window I looked down on the Sound of Bressay, as smooth as slate, on which the Bressay ferry might have scratched its wake diagonally across the roadstead.

At 3 o'clock in the afternoon, the wives of the teachers who lived in the houses on the campus, were sitting out in glorious sunshine at the front doors, whilst the bairns played happily in its pleasant warmth.

I was taking the boat south. As it was Thursday, I should be sailing on the *St Magnus*. In other circumstances, it would have offered an intriguing change from a return on the *Clair*. The *Magnus* was routed via Kirkwall, Orkney, then on to Aberdeen and Leith, instead of the direct run, Lerwick to Aberdeen.

By the time she was due to sail in the late evening, the icy northern blast of 12 hours earlier had warmed up and sprung up into a minor hurricane from the south-west! It wasn't long before the *Saint* was writing her name in the water, with firm plunges, artistic rolls and pitches forrard that would have done justice to ancient chronicles in Gothic script.

I draw a veil over my purgatory.

We made the harbour at Kirkwall in daylight. My mind was made up. The very thought of the crossing of the notorious Pentland Firth was enough to bring up what vestige of my supper remained for feeding the gulls. No doubt, in the lee of the N.E. mainland, things might have eased up. I wasn't risking it.

'Where is the office of the BEA (British European Airways as the line was known before it became BA)?' My head throbbed with the question. I still had to get ashore.

At the foot of the gangplank lay another danger to compound the perils of the night. The whole harbour area was a sheet of ice. I had already damaged my weak ankle in less serious conditions. A cat treading delicately on eggs was not it. Broad Street at last! Thank goodness!

My relief was short-lived. The wind had not died down. If anything it blew stronger than ever, for it was funnelled directly along Broad Street. I saw its strength right away. An elderly gent had walked out of a shop. Before he knew what was happening, the wind had whipped him yards along the street before he could wrest himself from its fury.

I reached the wall of the shop. Hugging to the window as close as I could, I reached along to the middle upright spar. Holding on, I moved slowly into the shop doorway. Glass - wood - doorway, from shop to shop, I made my way along the street. The BEA office was across the road. I made it!

"Have you any spare seats on the Aberdeen plane? I'm finished with the boat. You'd never get me back on board for all the tea in China."

There was a seat. To my delight, we flew smack over Fyvie Castle on the way into Dyce. I thought of an old Morgan colleague, Davie Donald, a mathematician as any Forfar loon worth his salt had to be, schooled by the brothers Thomson in the Academy. To his wife, Mary's accompaniment, he delighted folk far and wide, across to the USA with his singing of the ballads of his native Scotland. The *Bonnie Lass o' Fyvie* is one of my favourite songs.

It has only just struck me that all this trouble with the weather was due to equinoctial gales. It was that time of the year. We ought to have known better. Some of our furniture bore the brunt of it a couple of weeks later, on its journey north by sea. Skilful repairs were carried out by Mr Tait, the father-in-law of Alex 'Fishy' Fraser, who married Margaret, both good friends of ours from those days.

On one occasion, a gale kept me from an appearance with the Brass Band. They didn't miss me much at that performance. I don't even think *The Sound of Music* was on the programme; so, the audience would not have been robbed of the five bars that I usually managed to keep up with!

I had set out for the venue. A gale howled about King Harald and Harbour Streets. A baritone trumpet in its case is quite a bulky item to carry. I held it with my right hand. My left clung firmly to the low fancy-work of metal railing round our garden and No. 84's.

I turned the corner, still grasping the ironwork for dear life. A few more feet and its support came to an end. I was at the gable of the house, a smooth extent of wall with no handholds. Discretion is the better....!

I didn't dare take my hand away from the railing. There was nothing for it but to retrace my steps backwards! What a relief to be home in the shelter of our own doorway.

The interest of birds, feathered and other, is one that holds Shetlanders. The islands are famed for their sea-bird colonies. Bobby Tulloch has fostered the snowy owl. Fair Isle attracts bird watchers year after year.

We and the bairns especially, shall never forget the freak storm which tossed a host of gold crests into the streets of Lerwick. They were spattered and scattered into the fuschias, the privet and amongst the twisted sycamores. Folk gently picked up the pathetic creatures. Bairns brought them into school into the keeping of the science department. Much of their effort was in vain. The severity of the battering of the storm had weakened the tiny birds beyond their limit.

On one memorable occasion, our own human fledglings, and with them, their much bigger brothers and sisters, had to face blizzard conditions which taxed even the grown-ups.

The headmasters decided only to allow children home if they were accompanied by an adult.

Our youngest daughter was at the Bells Brae Primary school, just a few hundred yards away from home. So solid was the snow, driven by a strong north wind which found no obstacle to its course in our street, that mother could only make their return by walking backwards, sheltering the wee lass who had to walk backwards too. Facing the wind, they could not draw breath. It was a terrifying experience whilst it lasted.

Even senior pupils from the Institute found it frightening as they battled their way along the exposed section of road from the school to the more sheltered cover offered by the first houses.

Pupils naturally prayed for adverse conditions. Since the Institute was the only senior secondary school in Shetland, it had quite a lot of pupils who travelled fairly long distances daily into school. Warnings of adverse weather meant the closing of the school for that period. It was said, that pupils wanting a day off, would go onto the roof above the head's study when rain was falling, and empty buckets of water over his windows to try to lead him to believe weather conditions merited that freedom!

During our stay, the teaching associations and authorities were debating the institution of a four-term year. It was felt that time was being wasted after the 'Highers', as senior pupils 'free-wheeled' to the end of the school year. They had worked to their peak in order to gain the essential certificate, and, naturally, were loath to keep up the effort. How many of us grown-ups would feel any differently?

This post-exam time normally offered a chance for extra-mural activities which were not readily adaptable to the main part of the school year. School sports, operatics or concerts and visits to places of local interest could be fitted into this time.

'Oh, no!' said the voice of authority. 'You will need to fit such programmes into the main school year.'

So, it was suggested that a short June break would follow the exams and the new school-year would begin straight away after with a term of some nine weeks and then the summer hols. Term two would follow more or less the set pattern to Christmas, term three to Easter, and after that break, term four.

I had been involved in the discussions on the mainland before I came to Shetland and was in favour of the idea. Yet, I did not want the opportunity for the extra-mural interests to be forfeited. The new first term would be educational, but not too strictly tied to the exam programmes

In the Institute staffroom, I was 'shot down in flames'. What! Did a 'sooth-moother' not know that June is far from being the sunny month he could expect on the Scottish mainland? June is the month when the sea-mists roll in and blanket out the sun that knows no 'dim'. I could not argue against that. Nevertheless, during the June days of the 1966 seamen's strike, I never saw water so deeply blue, almost purple, in the summer sun. Even the Med could not rival it!

I ended my sojourn north of the 60° parallel at Eshaness, where I drove a couple of friends on a windy day to see the waves breaking against the bastion cliffs of that part of the mainland. They were duly impressed.

Yet, when I talk with Shetland friends of that time, they say that our spell was relatively calm. They had not known the weather so quiet as it was in that period from 1966 to 1969. By all accounts, it has been much worse since!

NATION MEETS WITH NATION

ONE COULD EASILY presume that the remoteness of Shetland would reveal a conservative, introspective community, out-moded in fashions, unconcerned with the events of the big world beyond its shores. Nothing could be further from the truth.

Quite an important part of the world actually came to Shetland, water-borne. These were the fishing-fleets of the European littoral outlining the limits of the North Sea. The flags of many nations fluttered at mast-heads: Norwegian, French, Dutch, Swedish, Danish, Icelandic, Spanish, German (West and the East Republic), Polish and Soviet, the latter operating through its Baltic ports.

The nationals of these countries might arrive in Lerwick as hospital cases, having suffered injury at sea in their hazardous career. Storm-bound fishermen came ashore to enjoy the rare tranquillity offered by a stable footing. Mechanical faults brought boats to harbour for repair. The Russians came for water!

The 'hammer and sickle' was hoisted over an independent fleet. Out at sea lay the factory-ship, taking aboard the herring catch of its drifters, to process and store it before heading for home to Tallinn and other Baltic ports. A powerful tug, equipped with precision lathes and workshop machinery, was on hand to carry out repairs, independent of foreign land-based yards. And tankers came alongside the Lerwick quays to take on board the thousands of gallons of water which were used in the factory-ship processing.

To anybody professing an interest in foreign languages, here was a marvellous opportunity to exercise that talent. It was one thing to be able to exchange greetings and the odd pleasantry. Much more satisfying and appreciated was the service of an interpreter at the hospital bedside of an injured fisherman. The skipper who was tied up with a mechanical problem, was only too glad to find someone who could explain the problem to the mechanic from the local repair shop.

Our senior pupils could be encouraged to make a start at practising their classroom learning in a foreign environment brought right to their door. This struck me as a solution to our post-exam problem.

The harbour was only five or ten minutes away from the school. It was a glorious June day. The class had a double period (an hour and a half) of French or German. Two West German 'loggers' were tied up in the harbour through mechanical trouble. I broached the matter with the Head. He gave his permission for us to go out of school, but not so whole-heartedly. He didn't know me well enough; but, he probably knew more about the nature of fishermen who had seen little of female company during a long fishing campaign! There are proportionately less boys in senior language classes also!

We stood alongside the *Dr Eichelbaum*, a real rust-bucket. The crew, mostly men in their late teens and early '20s, were not long in coming over to the rail. I introduced us and explained how good an opportunity this was for my pupils to be able to speak with real Germans. It was not long before shyness disappeared and haltingly, questions were asked and answered.

Then, a voice hailed me over to the deckhouse. It was the mate. I was shown into a very cramped cabin. With the German mate was his chief engineer and two other seamen. They were Russians, a similar duo. The fumes of vodka pervaded the close atmosphere. I was offered a glass, but had to decline. I had the responsibility of my job and it was still inside working hours! Orange juice was my tipple!

The presence of the Russians on this West German boat was most intriguing. It would have been more understandable if their guests had been from East Germany. I was able to learn a very important human lesson.

The tubing which conducted the compressed oil to the rams working the steering-gear was so rotten that there was not enough compression to allow the boat to be manoeuvred at the nets. The Russians were from the repair tug and were considering what could be done. In the end, I heard that they had replaced the complete tube circuitry for a bottle or two of schnapps.

And the lesson? For seafarers, the prime enemy is the SEA. No matter who is in difficulty, national political 'isms' go by the board. If the Russian engineers had not offered help then, when conditions were favourable, they might easily have found themselves called to a rescue in other more perilous circumstances.

As for the pupils, they were finding the young Germans keen to become friendly. Addresses were being exchanged. There were hints that they might meet ashore after school! One ardent German admirer was to track me down later, seeking my help to arrange a date!

I wonder what memories they have in Norden of that tête-à-tête in Lerwick. Twenty-six years on, I've looked up my address book. The name of Johnny, the chief engineer from the East Friesland Islands, is still clear in the 'B' section, one of the first names I wrote down there! And, six years ago, on a return visit to Shetland, I took the chance of teasing a certain lady about the advances that the young German had tried to make! She hadn't forgotten!

The pupils were not the only ones to gain leave of absence in situations needing a degree of linguistic ability.

An annual event was the arrival of the French Fishery Protection vessel, a craft of the French navy manned by a crew of 'pompons rouges'. The *Agile* arrived in port in September. There was a considerable fleet of French fishing-boats working the Shetland shoals. The *Agile* was there to keep 'Marianne's' eye on her nationals and ensure their welfare.

France had a representative in Shetland, the French Consular Agent, a highly respected Lerwick businessman, who had shipping interests, as his firm imported through its own fleet, various commodities, coal and household furnishings, and building materials, like timber and cement. He offered a warm invitation to the officers of the French ship to have lunch ashore in the Grand Hotel.

One morning I was invited to the head's room. I was quite unprepared for the way he received me.

"Donald, Frank Garriock has invited me to lunch with the French officers and he wants you to come along too. He'll be expecting you to act as interpreter and keep the party going!"

This was indeed a most pleasant surprise. In my Morgan days, I had had a similar experience with industrialists in the jute trade, when French jute-men from the Somme had visited Dundee to exchange views on their textile interests. These meetings, however, had taken place in an Easter holiday period! Arrangements for hospitality were similarly lavish.

One advantage of being in my profession was that I went to my work, dressed as one would expect a 'professional' to be. So, the pair of us left school just before the end of the morning session, in nice time to be on hand to assist at the introduction of Shetland hosts to their French guests.

An interpreter's job is no sinecure. It is less interesting over a meal. Whilst the majority of the diners are busily engaged with knife, fork, spoon or glass, there is always someone who wants to exchange an idea or a witticism. The dragoman either nibbles or finds himself having to swallow a tasty morsel with unseemly haste. More often than not, he finds his dish has turned cold!

I have a feeling that Frank had hinted that there would be time enough for chatting and that we should endeavour to enjoy the meal in comfort. There was time between courses for the social graces.

It is over the coffee and liqueurs that the fun really begins. Neither side readily appreciates that jokes, which often depend on a play of words, or on a good knowledge of the social habits of the opposite party, cannot always be translated satisfactorily. The point may be understood over an explanatory translating, but it loses bite.

Schoolboy jokes of the 'Knock! Knock! Who's there? — Peter! — Peter Who? — Peter Knight (before you go to bed)' are just as much lost as a French equivalent, asking for the name of a Japanese motorcyclist — 'Yamamoto Kidérape' (more correctly in French — 'Il y a ma moto qui dérape!' = 'There's my bike, skidding!')

There was one story I remember one of the jute wallahs relating, which did translate. The young schoolmistress was involving her class in the lesson on 'Fear'. In turn they were asked to come to the blackboard and draw something which would frighten her. One laddie drew a lion with open jaws, another drew a fierce tiger. A girl offered a crocodile. Wee Sandy, at the back of the room was gazing out of the window, evidently totally disinterested in the proceedings.

"Sandy, come to the front and let me see you draw something to frighten me."

Sandy traipsed to the front of the class, picked up the chalk and dabbed it on the board.

"Is that it?" asked the teacher.

"Yes," said Sandy. "That, Miss, is a period. You miss one of those ...!"

The crucial word sounds the same in both languages!

The officers of the *Agile* appreciated it.

In late afternoon, just in nice time to see the school dismiss, we were back. The hospitality had rendered me not quite 'hors de combat', but glad that I was not to be called on for teaching duty!

The day was not over. The *Agile* returned the compliment and we were invited aboard for a cocktail party in the evening. Wives were to accompany husbands.

September evenings in Shetland are hardly the time for convivial celebrations, at least, not in the manner as prepared by our French hosts. It was 'al fresco' and, at a later point, 'à la belle étoile'! The crew had rigged up an awning and side canvas on the after-deck. Electric multi-barred fires fought a losing battle against the northern chill. The dainties were most appetising, served by efficient orderlies from the mess. In no way could the complement of the *Agile* be faulted. Little by little, individuals made their way below to the warmth of the ward-room. A good time was being had by all.

We were sitting round the table. As often happens in such gatherings, I asked members of the crew which part of France they came from. The wireless operator was from Orleans, the twin town of Dundee. I knew the place quite well, having been involved with inter-city exchanges during my days in Morgan.

"I know Monsieur Duveau, the Orleans secretary of the twinning," I said.

"What? Old 'Clo-clo'? He was my teacher at the Ecole Normale!" said the wireless op.

'Clo-clo' was a nickname, derived clearly from Monsieur's first name, Clovis. A small world! But more was to follow.

A chief petty officer had seen wartime service and had been in Durban, South Africa.

"I suppose you dropped in at the Foyer des Forces Françaises Libres."

"Naturellement!" he replied.

I said no more. I got up, climbed the companion-way and made for home. I searched in my photo album, picked up a small passport-size photo and headed back to the ship.

The group was still conversing in the ward-room. I walked up to the CPO and handed him the snap.

"Well, I'll be blowed! Where did you get that?" he asked.

"At the Foyer, of course. An RAF pal of mine was half-French on his mother's side. We thought it would be a change to visit the Foyer. That's where we met Madame MacKenzie, the doyenne hostess for the day."

We were reminiscing on events of 23 years before! The wireless op burst in, "He knows everybody!"

An exaggeration, but it was remarkable that these contacts should be shared years after and thousands of miles apart!

There were less fortunate occasions when my French came in useful. Fishing is a hazardous life. Accidents on board often caused serious injury and the need for the casualty to be treated in the nearest hospital. This was Lerwick. Frank Garriock was pleased when I was able to stand in for him and interpret for the hospital staff. I could find time to visit during the evening hours. Once a patient was sufficiently mobile but not fully fit to return to his ship or, more often, return to France, he would spend some time at home with the family. We had warm invitations to call in whenever we were in France. It would have been fairly easy, as most of the fishermen came from Boulogne. I did have a chance, once, to call in at the offices of the fishing company. They were delighted to meet someone who knew Frank Garriock, who represented their interests in Shetland.

The *Vierge Marie*, a Boulogne boat found itself in trouble. As was my habit, I looked by the harbour to see if there was anything of interest in the way of foreign vessels. There she was, tied up alongside the quay. The harbour-master, Captain Inkster was on hand. "She's got a rope fouled round the prop. There's a diver down having a look at it. The skipper is concerned that, when the diver goes home for tea, he won't be back. He wants the job done as soon as possible, to get back to his fishing."

"OK. I'll have a word with the skipper."

I was able to assure him that the diver would be back and that I should be there, too, to help smooth things out if they needed my services. I'd be going home first for my own tea.

After tea, work progressed satisfactorily. For some inexplicable reason, I suddenly thought, "I wonder if these lads would be interested in a bit of Shetland lamb?" Sure thing!

The nearest butcher was the Norwegian, Syversen. There was no difficulty. We both went down to the boat and discovered they could take a couple of dozen lambs. Refrigeration was no problem. They had ice aboard for the catch!

There was an amusing side to the transaction. Quite a number of the crew had gone ashore. Unknown to them, their mates were ordering lambs or offering to take a share in one. Imagine the effect on a none too sober Frenchman, when he was told he owned a part or the whole of a Shetland lamb! There was a sequel to the story. Some months later, I just happened to reach the quay, again on my way home for tea. The *Vierge Marie* had cast off and was moving away. On the after-deck stood one of the lamb-buyers.

"How did you get on with the lambs?"

"Great! But, we had some problems trying to hide them from the Customs. One of the lads had a great reception. His lamb was the centre of the table at a wedding reception of one of his daughters!"

That wasn't the only lamb episode. One Saturday morning, I was hardly out of bed, when the phone rang. It was a Mr Hunter. Could I help out? He had a Frenchman in the office who was keen to buy some Shetland sheep.

"Hold on," I answered. "Give me a moment to get a bite of breakfast and I'll be along."

Monsieur Ferioli and his wife were keen to buy sheep. They had already run a flock of Shetland sheep for some time. Inbreeding was leading to a need for fresh blood. I was interested to learn that Le Vexin, a region north of Paris, Monsieur's farming area, offered many of the characteristics of the Shetland scene, which suited the Shetland type of sheep. On lush pasture they tend to lose their familiar traits. Monsieur was keen to preserve them.

Readers may wonder how a teacher, limited more or less to textbook French, deals with technical language. His knowledge of the language means he can ask relevant questions, use gestures or make drawings, eventually hearing the word or expression he needs.

The difficulty arose, as the Feriolis enquired about the health of the flock they were interested in buying. Foot and Mouth Disease was something they needed to be sure about. 'La fièvre aphteuse'.

The 'fièvre' bit was understandable, but, what kind of a fever was it? I'd never heard the word 'aphteuse'! Madame came to my aid with a couple of simple gestures. She pointed to her mouth and feet!

I was reminded on another occasion, in Brittany, when another agricultural scourge made its appearance.

My Breton friend, Max and I were walking along the road, when Max pointed to a beetle-like insect crawling across in front of us. I should never have noticed it. Max used the telling French phrase which hinted that I had my eyes in my pockets! Pointing to the insect, he exclaimed, "Un doryphore!" He went on to say that it attacked potato crops. I'd never seen the creature, but I had heard of the Colorado beetle. Perhaps the destructive nature of the disease and the insect impressed on me the importance of the French words, so that I still remember them.

Answering the early morning call to Mr Hunter's had its reward. The Feriolis invited me to lunch. I thanked them but had to decline for some family reason. A parcel was later delivered to our house with Mr Hunter's compliments. It was a delicious lamb roast!

German was another string to my bow, but its arrow was not quite so penetrating as the French! Nevertheless, it played its part in a roundabout way, when a fleet of Polish fishing-boats took shelter in Lerwick.

During the war, my wife's folk had given hospitality to a Polish serviceman, based near their home. Kazik had acquired some English. When he returned to his native Poland, contact was kept up through an annual Christmas card.

Whilst they rested from the storm, the Polish fishermen came ashore. Poor lads, they were not only handicapped by the language, but by the lack of hard currency too. They found an answer to this latter problem. When they went into town, they were very warmly clad, wearing umpteen shirts, one on top of the other. All but the last were for sale. A buyer suddenly saw his salesmen doing a minor striptease, as he was handed the shirt of his choice!

My curiosity was aroused, because it dawned on me that they might have known something about the area where Kazik came from. I was invited on board. Then, to my surprise, I found myself conversing with one of the crewmen in German.

I explained about Kazik.

"Write a letter to him in German and bring it to me. I'll translate it into Polish and you can send it off."

Right away I dashed back home. My wife dictated the message in English. I did the translation and went back aboard the Polish boat. Some time later my Polish friend handed me the copy in his language. It was beautifully written, in twirls and curls, in violet ink. I was delighted.

The outcome was also surprising. The letter had gone to Bartoszyce, a town which had been in East Prussia, in pre-war days. Kazik's wife was replying ... in German! From that moment on, the contact, though still restricted to an annual exchange, now was lengthier, turned into a letter. Mrs Kazik explained that it was very difficult to find anybody in the district who knew English. German must have survived from its historical background.

There was a period in the 1970s when life was especially hard in Poland. Poles, who had settled in this country, decided to do their utmost for their fellow countrymen. Mr Korunka, a businessman in Kinross, organised through his own transport fleet, a series of deliveries of medical, food and clothing supplies to his native Poland. We were able to send a parcel of items to Kazik's widow, thanks to this organisation. Later, we learnt from her, that there were problems on her side. The Communist hierarchy were staking claims to parcels that didn't belong to them. Thanking us, she begged us to send no more!

The Soviet water-tanker, *Kandagach*, was such a regular caller in Lerwick, that many of its crew members were in the habit of strolling about the town. Some years earlier, I, like many other language teachers, had attended night classes in Russian, arranged by the Dundee authority, in the University buildings. A government directive encouraged the learning of Russian to meet future needs, as the USSR was opening out to the West. Classics teachers were also wooed. Their highly inflected languages offered a good basis for learning the new subject. The Greek script was an added bonus!

One Sunday afternoon, I met with the chief engineer and his radio operator from the *Kandagach*. I invited them up home. It was quite an entertaining session, even for the bairns. With my limited vocabulary and pencil and paper, we still learned quite a bit about each other's families, for they were family men.

We had tea and cakes. The wireless operator had some English. It was standard practice, for a knowledge of English was essential in passing international calls for help at sea. I offered them a run in the car. Out Weisdale way, near the war memorial, we stopped to have a look round. Sheep were grazing all around. There may have been a ram amongst them. At all events, I crouched down and cupped my hands round my ears to imitate the animal. The answer came ... 'Baran'!

Back at King Harald Street, we had more chat. The lampshade in the kitchen had a camel motif round its rim. The chief came from Kazakhstan, hundreds, if not thousands of miles from the sea.

That astonished me. It would have made more sense, in a way, if he had come from Murmansk or Odessa. One could imagine then, a link with the sea and a desire to be a seafarer. Still surprising, yet more understandable, was the sight of his finger pointing to the lampshade. Quite excitedly, he said, "Verbleyod!' Camels were a familiar sight to him. He must have seen convoys of the 'ships of the desert' in his part of the Soviet Union.

We all walked back with them to their ship. Chief made signs for us to come on board. The bairns were most reluctant. In their mind's eye, they saw their Dad being shanghaied across the sea. I reassured them.

The chief's cabin was snug and comfortably furnished. He offered us hunks of very fatty pork and Georgian wine to wash it down. Then he led us to an entertainment room to see a film, boy meets girl and they live happily ever after in the care of the Communist state.

One feature that attracted my comment when we were back at home, was the presence of quite a number of women in the crew. This was not a pleasure-cruise liner. It was a working ship. No doubt, there were many more women on the factory ship, where the gutting of the fish and other operations would be their duty.

Fraternising with representatives from the Eastern Bloc was not confined to us grown-ups. A training-ship from Estonia put in, manned by a crew of young cadets. This gave our soccer team from the AEI an opportunity to entertain the young Estonians.

Later, in the evening, we were invited on board to play billiards! BILLIARDS, aboard ship? Well, it was a game played with cues! The 'balls' were flat, little square wooden blocks. In an effort to converse with the officers, I scanned the pages of a Russian phrase-book that Doug Smith had used to help him qualify in Russian. Much laughter answered my pointing to the word 'Shoot' on one page and 'the referee' on another!

Really, there was something very special about the atmosphere in Lerwick and elsewhere in Shetland. The presence of those Soviet citizens, moving so freely amongst us, despite the Cold War in the bigger world, was proof of that. Perhaps, we all learned a little about international understanding from those contacts and try, in our lives today, to break down the barriers.

Before I left Shetland, Mr Laurenson ('Peerie Ertie') of the Harbour Authority, presented me with a book token for services rendered. The exchange I made has proved apt and most useful, especially now in my retirement. Crosswords and writing are an absorbing interest. So, sincere thanks to Mr Laurenson and his Board and Mr Roget for his Thesaurus. It contains words from all over the globe which are now part and parcel of our rich language.

TWENTY-FIVE YEARS ON

I HAD a sudden thought this morning about my Shetland item. I didn't mention the day when the Norwegian veterans returned to celebrate the 25th anniversary of the Shetland Bus. That was a day very special to Shetland folk, unlikely to be celebrated anywhere else, unless in Norway.

Well, there was a Norwegian dimension to it, because the Norwegian Government assembled all the veterans from wherever they were living in the country and transported them to the dock for the voyage to Lerwick, expenses paid.

Fred Olsen, the shipping magnate, had put one of his vessels at the disposal of the government. She was the *Leda*, a much bigger vessel than the *Clair*. She was a cruise ship, scheduled to sail the world's oceans.

That early summer's morning, the whole town of Lerwick and many of the folk from the countryside were agog with excitement, as the hour of the *Leda*'s arrival approached. Though we were outsiders, our emotions were equally stirred. We had lived through the war years and both of us had seen service away from home with His Majesty's forces. I had been overseas.

The details of the arrival are misty; but I shall never forget the glow on the face of a Burra lass, when, in the throng, she spotted the farthest-travelled of the contingent, a veteran from Nord Kapp. He had a round, open face and was amazed and delighted to meet her again.

They had danced at parties in the local halls, as young folk, twenty-five years before. No doubt, her folk had shown him and others of his compatriots traditional Shetland hospitality in the home. Nor must we forget that Shetland menfolk were away to the war, where their skill with boats landed them in such services as mine-sweeping our own coastlines. Nothing was more natural than that the absence of the local young men should encourage the youth of allied nations to fraternise. The proof is to be seen in Norwegian families were Mum is from Shetland, and in Shetland, where Dad is of Norwegian birth.

Suddenly, we were swallowed up in a mêlée of hugging couples. Norse greetings rushed from Shetland lips. Norwegian veterans lilted English answers. I could almost feel myself lost in a frenzy of 'Geordie' home-coming! 'Come away hjem, man!'

The man from Nord Kapp interested me particularly, because on that very point of the Norwegian coast, my Dad, was shipwrecked on his first voyage at the time of the First World War!

I became involved in the celebrations because the welcoming committee wanted folk, who had cars, to be available to drive the veterans about the place.

Two chaps I picked up were keen to go over to Scalloway, where they had been based. I kept in touch with Georg Holmen of Oslo and Jacob Silden from Måløy (Lerwick's twin town) for a while afterwards by letter, trying out my new knowledge of the Norwegian I was in the process of learning. Jacob was working with SAS (Scandinavian Airways) if I remember rightly.

Group by group, veterans and their Shetland hosts made their way back to the harbour. The sight-seeing was over. The guests were now to become the hosts. The *Leda* was a floating hotel and clubroom non-stop for the remaining hours of the twenty-four. It had certainly been a true, long summer's day. Having less part in it, we went home to be up and ready to wave farewell in the morning.

Most of the Shetlanders didn't go to bed until after the ship sailed. They had entertained the Norwegians ashore and then had accepted hospitality on board for the rest of the night.

It was a grey morning when the ropes were cast off. Hats and hankies waved. Farewells were shouted. Voices died away. Eyes strained to see the last outlines of figures, once young and eager. The *Leda* disappeared behind the Knab. A strange quietness descended on the huddles of folk, suddenly aware that they had not slept a wink. What were their dreams?

How many a 'Husker du ...?' (D'you remember ...?) passed among those, sailing hjemover?

INNOCENTS(?) ABROAD

ONE MORNING, just weeks after my arrival, I received in the school mail a letter from a French address. It was written in English of a sort, hard to decipher. We later learned that a number of similar letters had been sent off, in the hope that one might be answered. Some party of the Vosges département was looking to arrange an inter-school exchange. This was a challenge and an opportunity to provide the local children with something that their remoteness made very difficult. It was a tiring enough task carrying out an exchange with Orleans from Dundee. In Lerwick we were 250 miles or so further away.

I broached the matter with the Head. Having ultimate responsibility, he was wary of committing himself or his staff, especially as I was new to the post, but not to the task. If there had been any opposition, however, I had a strong ally in no less a person than the Director of Education who had interviewed me in the first place. He had a special interest in the success of such a mission. Two of his children were pupils in the senior school and proficient in French. My superiors discussed the matter. I was given permission to go ahead.

Cost is a major factor in these expeditions. We were to fly from Sumburgh to Aberdeen. There it would be by rail to Dover, a cross-Channel boat and the SNCF (French Rail) to our destination in eastern France. It is an advantage to have a large enough group so that travel concessions are available. Specialist travel companies offer free travel and accommodation to leaders of the party on the basis of one free to 10 pupils. Ours was to be self-organised. French Rail offered a similar concession for the travel part, as we had more than 10 pupils interested. Accommodation was not a problem, since we were making an exchange and would therefore entertain our hosts when it was their turn to come to Shetland.

What made the trip possible for the Shetland youngsters was the generosity of the Authority to pay for the air travel from Shetland and the return. It wasn't the flight that intrigued the pupils. Many were old hands at flying. But, seldom had they travelled by rail! No railway service exists in the islands.

This was brought home to the Ministry of War, when servicemen applied for travel warrants from their bases in Shetland. Each request for a rail ticket had to have the name of the nearest railway station marked on it. RAF personnel stationed at Scatsta, a Coastal Command station on Sullom Voe, took out their charts and measured the distance from base to Wick and base to Bergen. Their request went forward, marked 'Bergen, Norwegian State Railway'!

At Aberdeen, we were joined by two pupils from the Kingussie School of my former Morgan colleague, whose experiences in his new job had taken me to

Lerwick! It was a wearying journey with the first night on the mainland spent travelling to London. The resilience of youth makes light of such matters. We still had a long way to go with changes across London and also in Paris, though the Gare de l'Est is closer to the Gare du Nord than Kings Cross to Victoria!

Despite many journeys in France, I never fail to enjoy the sight of that country and the pleasure of pointing out to newcomers the white eminence of the Sacré Coeur, as the train approaches Paris. And there are so many things so different to be seen in France, that a teacher is kept on his toes, explaining this, pointing out that, getting that special feel of the atmosphere, the smell of 'Gitanes', of garlic in the salami of family picnics in the compartments or corridors and, less attractive, the odour of the toilettes!

Our train journey ended at Epinal. It was only then that we learned of a change of plans. Our hostel base for the stay was not available. Instead of being just a few kilometres away, we were to travel quite a distance by bus up into the wooded slopes of the Vosges mountains. It was a very tired group which stepped down from the coach at a large chalet-type building in the heart of pine forest.

Our hostess was Madame Henner, the wife of Charles, who ran the Vosges system of 'Colonies de Vacances'. Schools close for long summer holidays in France. Why not put the buildings to use in that time? Many secondary schools in rural areas are equipped with dormitories and refectories, as many of their scholars are obliged to live away from home, so they are ideally suited to provide accommodation, much as a youth hostel would do.

The staff often consists of a teacher and kitchen employees. His family can share the holiday with him. Town children have an opportunity to live in the country. The Vosges office has 'colonies' on the Atlantic and Mediterranean coasts, so that children who may never have seen the sea, are able to spend an excitingly new holiday at a seaside resort in a school building in that place. Children of the Vosges mountains and valleys can exchange places and learn something of each others environment and way of life.

Our chalet was really designed for younger children of primary school. Yet, we could not complain. We ate well. We needed no rocking that night.

I expected some reaction from my band when they awoke to see the forest clearer in daylight. Nothing! Trees are almost non-existent in Shetland. Those that are readily seen in and about Lerwick are stunted and twisted in their battle against the violent winds and the driving salt spray.

Here, by our hillside meadow, trees rose tall and straight. I had the impression that the young Shetlanders felt at home. Then it dawned on me. The steady soughing of the wind in the branches reminded them of the constant breaking of the waves on the shore or against the cliffs of home.

A few days later, we had to move out to make room for the intended guests, bairns from four to nine years old with their helpers. They trooped in, paired off, holding hands, singing some well-known folk song, a joyous band, ready to enjoy a wonderful holiday surprise.

Our new home was a massive building, in the plain, at the centre of the small township of Jarménil. Inter-town exchanges had meant the pairing off of participants, the host taking his guest into his own home. Accompanying teachers might be housed in a similar way, or, as did happen in Orleans, have a flat offered to them. Their main task was to be on hand to solve any problems and escort the group on cultural visits in the region.

In such exchanges, the main problem was to find a suitable partner. Application forms gave details of sex, age, interests and family background. It was hoped that a doctor's 18-year-old son, keen on fishing, would be happy in the company of a teacher's 16-year-old boy, with an interest in ornithology, if those were the nearest details for a pairing. It has always amazed me how so many exchanges, so arbitrarily thrown together, not only stuck it out, but kept up the friendship and have done so into the following generation.

In Jarménil Charles Henner had another idea. Our home was the regional youth centre, set in extensive grounds, which bordered the infant river Moselle. We were to share the spacious building with our French hosts, amongst whom were the Henner children, aged from 11 to 19. They brought some of their teenage pals to make up numbers. Two cooks, who joined us on some of our outings, saw to our gastronomic needs, and expertly.

To give us extra freedom, though this caused me some concern, Charles provided a fleet of brand-new bikes. I had my doubts about letting our youngsters cycle on the 'wrong' side of the road. Fortunately, we were slightly off the beaten track. The cycles proved a boon.

One of the highlights of the visit was a session at a 'Ranch', where the Shetlanders, mounted on horseback, followed a woodland trail. On the way back to base, they discovered a skittle-alley at the back of an auberge. The bowls rolled as satisfyingly down the 'piste' as the light ale down their throats!

Below the centre were cellar vaults with walls feet thick. Though we were in the centre of the town and pop music was going full blast into the wee sma' oors, as lads and lasses rocked and jived, nobody was disturbed. It was a freedom groups would rarely know on other stereotyped exchanges.

A day's walk and picnic in the Vosges forest, a visit to an historical centenary in Remiremont, with characters dressed in the garb of the time, a sampling of Vittel spa water and a visit to the bottling-plant, which shuffled a million bottles through the system per week, plus a firework display, lighting up the sky above and around the spire of Strasbourg Cathedral on the 14th July, must live long in the memories of our wanderers. A salute to 'Le Pêcheur' would not come amiss! He was the figure on the lager bottles, the contents of which consoled us in our long hours of waiting for the train home on that last day!

A year later, we were the hosts.

It is hard to imagine how the Vosgiens found their trip to Lerwick. In their homeland, they were hundreds of miles from the nearest sea. The voyage from Aberdeen was almost as long as any train journey they might have made from home to the Atlantic or the Med. The chances are, that at the end of those journeys, they would have disembarked on the platform of Nice or Granville in glorious sunshine.

Arrival at 8am at Lerwick in the month of July can be completely different. It was! The air was cool, the sky grey, rain threatening. The grey stone of the town was not encouraging. And they were cold. They had come ill-prepared for the maritime climate above 60 degrees North latitude! French shorts (and they are short!), short-sleeved T-shirts, socks and light sandals offered little warmth and protection against a steady sea-breeze.

Luckily, the next day dawned warm and bright, not a cloud in sight. The sun had already been doing its stuff from about 2am! We would go to Sumburgh, visit Jarlshof with all its archaeological interest and enjoy a picnic on a lovely sandy beach.

The new residents, Mr & Mrs Smith, in the summer of 1966 outside 82 King Harald Street, Lerwick.

Jessie Irvine of Gulberwick. The author and his family met her in 1958 travelling north on the "St Clair" and have remained in touch ever since.

Shetland-bound. Hilary and Merilyn aboard the "St Clair" in July 1958.

The first exchange group in the Vosges at Jarménil in July 1966. Left to right: D. B. Smith, Frances Cheyne, Ann Robertson, Fiona Wishart, Alan Gifford, Kirsten Davidson, Victor Lockwood, ?, Jonathan Wordsworth, Annette Bald, Yvonne Drever, Jean Anderson and Elizabeth Wordsworth. Jonathan and Elizabeth Wordsworth were pupils from Kingussie who joined the Shetland party. They are descendants of the famous poet, William Wordsworth.

AEI staff photo 1966-67. Back row: Garry Williamson, Tom Robinson, Reggie Williamson, Laurence Moncrieff, John Tait, George Black, Robert Ollason, ? French assistant. Middle row: Ellen Irvine, Donald Macdonald, Lorna Ward, Laurence Graham, Adelaide Manson, George Jamieson, Margaret Isbister, Jim Coull, Patricia Johnson. Front row: William Thomson, Mary Garrick, John Graham, Miss Andrew, William Rhind, Agnes Robertson, Angus Laurenson, Elizabeth J. Henry, Donald B. Smith.

Photo: © Dennis Coutts

AEI Sixth Year 1966-67. Back row: Alistair Mullay, Jan Borthwick, Jack Greenwald, Peter Leask, Andrew Johnson, Jim Moncrieff, Maurice Smith, Norman Leask, Jim Tait. 2nd row: Douglas Johnstone, Graham Sutherland, Alexander Laurenson, Andrew Spence, John Strachan, Jim Johnson, Robin Barclay, Colin Stove, Frank Hay, Martin Moncrieff, Angus Jamieson. 3rd row: Laureen Couper, Christine Manson, Winifred Leask, Janet Longston, Ann Spence, June Robertson, Isobel Sutherland, Joan Dargie, Christine Ratter, Emmie Smith, Pat Moar, Agnes Hansen. Front row: Margaret Leask, Lorraine Malcolmson, Yvonne Henderson, Georgia Smith, Valerie Jamieson, Barbara Berry, Jean Anderson, Iris Isbister, Elizabeth Peterson, June Peterson.

Photo: © Dennis Coutts

Senior pupils from the AEI pose for the camera during their long weekend at Voe with French assistante, Michèle Cabille. Back row: Marion Irvine, Marcelle Cadenhead, Merilyn Smith, Margaret Bulter, June Leask, Jessie Watt. Front row: Pat Moar, Jean Johnson, Ann Williamson, Veronica Slater, Ann Bain, Rosemary Mallace, Mademoiselle Cabille and Fiona Wishart.

The author near the Morrisons' croft at Swining Voe in September 1967 with his wife and daughter, Hilary.

The "Venture" anchored at Hamnavoe. The author's trips to the fishing and his friendship with the Burra crew are recalled in this book.

French assistante Mademoiselle Michèle Cabille and D. B.'s French pal Henri Roche with Soviet crew aboard a Soviet trawler.

Joe Laurenson returns the author's family and friends to Quarff after a visit to Bridge-End.

On board the "Agile" Bill Rhind, Donald B. Smith, Jane Spence and Kay Garriock with a crew member. In the background are Magnus Shearer, Frank Garriock and the author's daughter, Hilary

The 1969 school trip stopped at Dundee railway station to pick up victuals, supplied by friends of the author, for the onward journey to Dieppe. The party were able to spend a few days, including Bastille Day, in Paris. Back row: Flo and Charlie Aitken, John Ollason, Adelaide Manson, D. B. Smith, John Tulloch, Valerie McQueen, Hilary Smith, Jean Couper, Ronnie Smith, Frances Ollason, Susan Davison, Joyce Thomson, Margaret Tulloch, Jane Nicolson, Fiona Kerr, Odette Black. Front row: Jim Tait, Frank Miller, Moira Rendall, Iain Hastings, Kay Hunter, Beatrice Wishart, Thelma Johnson, Doris Pottinger, Irene Sandison, Louise Gordon.

Photo: © D. C. Thomson & Co. Ltd.

Mr & Mrs Smith visit their friends from the croft at Swining Voe, brother and sister Lawrie and Jean Morrison, who now live at Vidlin.

WANTED:

Principal
teacher of French – opportunities
to speak Norwegian and Russian

ZETLAND EDUCATION COMMITTEE

Applications are invited from Registered Teachers for appointment as Principal Teacher of French at the Anderson Educational Institute, Lerwick, presently a Senior Secondary School but shortly to become a six-year all-through Comprehensive School. Salary National Scale plus £380 in respect of responsibility and island service. A seven-apartment house is available at moderate rental. Removal expenses will be paid. Applications should be made to the Director of Education, Education Offices, Brentham Place, Lerwick, Shetland, within 10 days of the appearance of this advertisement.

A principal teacher of French is required for one of Scotland's most northerly schools, according to this reproduction of an advertisement which appeared in last week's issue of the Journal. With the consent of the Rector of the Anderson Educational Institute, and of the Director of Education for Zetland, the present holder of the post has written this article in "an effort to persuade someone that the post is very much a worthwhile one".

VENTURE. This is the name of a Shetland fishing-boat, officially registered as LK 337, an apt name for a successful Burra boat and a fitting theme for this challenging appeal to you who may follow in my footsteps.

For three and a half years I have been head of the French department in the Anderson Educational Institute.

By Donald B Smith

Lerwick, and now we are returning to the mainland to be near our parents who are in their late 70's. This is a problem that has to be faced. Three and a half years ago we leaped into the middle of the North Sea without much forethought, but now in retrospect, without any regrets.

As a family we had spent a holiday in the wilds of Shetland 11 years ago. Though enjoying the holiday, I was quite sure I could never live in "that god-forsaken spot". These were my words as I gazed at the fertile Mearns and Strathmore on our return journey to Dundee. So when the post became vacant in December 1965, my answer was categoric — "I wouldn't uproot the family to go to such a place".

But after 18 years in one post and wanting to run my own show, it seems I only needed a little encouragement — retired parents making the unexpected remark: "You can be too long in one spot and taken for granted", and the more positive enthusiasm of a former colleague, promoted to a Highland school where he was boss of his own show with couthie kids to teach, discipline no problem, and outside of school a lively

social life to be enjoyed. So three phone calls later, plus an interview on my own lounge carpet, I was offered the post!

What did we find? First, a roomy house in Lerwick within a few hundred yards of everything — shops, pubs, cinema, theatre, library, kirk, school and harbour. Within a week I was widely known, though I hardly knew a soul!

In the same week I had been invited to join the brass band, on the call from across the street of a complete stranger who had heard I had some interest in music. One contact has led to another, so that by the end of the stay, my wife has been involved in work with the Guides, Red Cross, the Arts and Crafts Guild and innumberable coffee mornings, while our daughters have found outlets for their energies in drama, choirs, orchestra, Brownies and country dancing as well as hockey and netball (with opportunities to represent Shetland in the inter-county competitions).

I have found a practical outlet for my academic learning as an interpreter to the Harbour Authority, hospital, banks and the Shetland wool trade and the Tourist Office. In four summers I have had more opportunities to speak French in Shetland than I should ever have had on the mainland.

With an almost daily contact with Norway through the harbour, I set about acquiring a knowledge of Norwegian and now have a "Higher" in it! If I were younger and more determined, Russian would be my next goal, as there is a daily need for it in the port.

Our chief regret is that we did not come 10 years earlier. This is really an appeal to a young family, whose children can be assured of a first class education through primary and secondary school. Children will find a freedom that our generation knew 40 years ago. All will find a rhythm of life that is natural and relaxing. You yourself will be teaching in a modern school, to be enlarged and equipped with a language laboratory in two years' time. Your colleagues are young and energetic. The local authority will give you every encouragement to take groups abroad. (In 1966 we went to the Vosges and entertained the Vosgiens in Shetland in 1967. This year we had a wonderful summer trip to Dieppe and Paris).

There are snags. A climate that can allow such weather changes as warm spring sun, three inches of snow, a howling northerly gale, a flat calm and a Force 10 gale from the south, all inside 36 hours, is something to be reckoned with.

But this is the exception. I should rather judge it by the fact that seldom have I worn a top-coat during our stay here, and more often, summer and winter alike, have I gone out in a sports jacket.

The housewife will complain at the higher prices of most foodstuffs, but if she acquires a deep-freeze, she will make big savings on meat, fish and poultry, all of prime quality.

Medical services are good, with a bright, attractively situated hospital recently built. The dental services are under pressure, though the school dental corps offers a first-rate service, readily available to its young patients.

If you are prepared to "venture", you will find by the end of your stay that you will have broadened your horizons, made some very good friends and acquired a good professional training that will be useful in further promotion. You won't regret coming, but you will certainly have regrets on leaving.

Article by D. B. Smith in the "Scottish Educational Journal" issue dated 12th September, 1969.

– viii –

The sea looked most tempting, an unbelievable blue, almost verging on purple in its intensity. The Henner boys would lead the way. Clad solely in their even shorter trunks, they dashed across the golden sand, warm underfoot. It was good to be alive on such a day in such surroundings, with admiring young Shetland girls cheering their dashing ways.

Jacqui rushed into the blue, threw himself into the waves. Next second, he was upright, beating a hasty goose-pimpled retreat back to the warmth and shelter of the sand-dune where he had stripped for a swim! Instead of the 22°C normally registered in the Med, he had felt the sting of something nearer 10°C in the North Sea. His teeth chattered uncontrollably through a sandwich!

Our Vosgiens friends enjoyed highlights in their stay. The Bressay ferryman had a boat for hire which took keen sea-fishermen off The Bard. We hired an evening of his services. He provided bait and lines, but no warm outer clothing!

Perhaps the excitement of hooking ling or piltock made our friends forget the chill. In quieter moments, they shrank into the warm space near the wheelhouse and the heat from the motor. I had no success with the line, but the bronzed red of the sunset is unforgettable. A strip of 8mm cine film has registered it for years to come.

The sea too was to provide a wonderful spectacle. A school of porpoises ('neesicks' in the Shetland tongue) arched their way in formation just yards from the boat, drawing our fisherlads and lasses to the rail in admiration.

Our Shetland remoteness gave us an opportunity for a novel treasure hunt. Car-owning colleagues were called in to lend a hand. Arrangements were made with postmasters in post-offices in the hinterland to act as marshals. The plan was to take Shetlanders and Vosgiens, paired off together, to a point some twenty miles from Lerwick, north, south and west. (There isn't enough land east!) There they would be dropped off and left to find their own way back by whatever means, passing through the check-points at village post-offices on their route. Who would be the first home?

Nothing like it could have been done in the Vosges. Some of our comely lasses might have landed in a camel-train in the Arabian Desert. For others, it might have been 'Vladivostock, here we come!'

It was a test of ingenuity and proof of the friendliness of Shetland folk. The competitors arrived back at base, some as black as the ace of spades, having helped to deliver coals for a trip home. One hung on to the side of a tractor cab for a few miles. The tractor was the only vehicle on that section of the road! Each one had a tale of success or failure. It was voted a great idea.

As in Jarménil, we declared 'open house'. Our original travellers brought their pals in to join our French guests, just as the Henners had done in France. We used the school as the base.

There were no dormitory facilities in the school. The hostels nearby would have been ideal for that. We managed to bed everyone down on camp-beds and the like. The canteen staff of normal school days rallied round and valiantly strove to satisfy the appetites of the bunch. I had grossly miscalculated the expense of their services, as the participants in the exchange were expected to pay enough to cover costs. In the end, the Authority footed the bill.

The school was far enough away from the last houses in that part of the town for us to feel that we could repeat the 'rock' sessions of Jarménil and rock, most literally, 'round-the-clock'! Though my section of the old school had rooms below school level, they were not below ground, like cellars. So, the lights blazed on into the night. (In August the days are beginning to shorten appreciably.) Notice of this was being taken by officials and questions being asked!

I think allowances were made, for this had been an experiment and lessons were there for the learning. Other trips to France followed, but in a more conventional way, though we were able to use the 'Colonie de Vacances' establishments along the Norman coast and in Paris, living our own routine with little interference from officialdom.

Dieppe was one of our destinations. Its lycée where we stayed is situated on the cliff-top south of the town. It was a spacious modern building, so that we found ourselves sharing accommodation with a group of younger pupils of a school from the south of England.

I think that there were hints made that it had been built in a hurry and there had been some cost-cutting. Something was far from right in the ablution section. Showers, hand-basins and toilets were available for large groups of pupils, both local French boys and visitors.

The plumbing was rather complicated. Piping hot water came through the shower-roses all right; but the turning-off caused problems. Either, we had misunderstood the instructions or, the plumber had misread the drawings. After the showers had been in use, we became aware of a pleasant warmth in the toilet-pans, when we had recourse to that section of the block. Somehow, the hot water from the showers was filling the cisterns in the toilets. The warmth may have helped those whose regularity was a difficulty! At any rate, nobody asked for 'Ex-lax' tablets!

For our young Shetlanders, Dieppe had a 'star' attraction, its Olympic-sized, open air, heated swimming-pool, with attendant installations for 'thalassathérapie'.

I had to look that one up in the dictionary! I learned that the therapy coming from 'thalassa' was simply brine-baths. The imposing first half of the word was quite simply Greek for 'sea'!

Thirty years slipped away in a twinkling, as I recalled Kinglake's *Eothen*, one of our set books for the Matriculation English exam. 'Thalassa! Thalassa! The sea! The sea!' The author had topped a rise in the ground in Asia Minor and was looking down on the Eastern Med!

The word cropped up again in Lerwick Harbour. The fishery research vessel of East Germany berthed with us for a spell. Her name was fittingly *Thalassa*!

Though Dieppe was our base, we managed to spend a couple of days in Paris. We were living on a shoe-string. How was I going to ensure we had adequate lunches? We had wandered into a little square, a backwater in the Quartier Latin. There was a bistro and shops. I sent some of the pupils out to buy bread, cheese, tomatoes and fruit. We came back to the 'terrasse' of the bistro, where those of us who had stopped, had arranged tables and chairs to keep the group together. Then, I explained:

"In France, there are pubs which allow you to bring your own eats, provided that you buy their refreshments. This is just such a pub!"

We lunched quite satisfactorily!

We 'did' Paris as best we could. The top of the Eiffel Tower was out! There are enough problems in getting up to the first floor, even out of season. On our visit to Versailles, we 'lost' the youngest member of the party. He had failed to follow instructions for returning to a rendezvous point! He turned up later, blithely unconcerned, but feeling a bit worse for wear. He had not been able to resist the cheapness of fresh fruit and had over-indulged!

Naturally, our sight-seeing involved quite a bit of travel in the city. We took the 'Métro'. Before rush hour we had perfected a system of getting everyone off at the right station.

Two of the senior lads were posted by one of the doors of the carriage. The call-sign was 'Up-Helly-A". It resounded through the coach at the station before our stop. The doors opened. 24 youthful figures darted out and lined up immediately against the station wall. Adelaide, my co-leader, ran along the row. '24! All present and correct!'

We performed this ritual on a rush-hour train, crammed to the doors. Our folk were intrigued to read the sign on the coaches – 'Seats for 24, Standing 118!' And the first four places were for expectant mothers, war-wounded and disabled folk.

The gentleman seated next to me took exception to the war-cry. His breath smelt strongly of alcohol. I offered an explanation, pointing out that discipline was important in such situations. I added that I had learned some of it in the RAF. The moment I mentioned those three letters, his attitude changed immediately. He was my blood brother from then on!

As they say, 'All good things come to an end.' That end, however was almost a thousand miles away. In between, was the prospect of a Customs inspection. I warned them all that none of them were old enough to carry back tobacco or alcohol. I was hoping to avoid an inspection. A cousin was in the service on one of the Channel ports, where most of the officials were known to each other. I had used his name as a password on earlier school trips from Dundee.

It worked again. We passed through in a twinkling.

The homeward train journey was long. Morning saw us crossing the Forth Bridge at an early hour. The dawn tinged the sky with a rosy light. A thin film of mist hung over the river. My cine-camera whirred. It came out as a perfect sequence on the film.

The young folk were waking up. I went amongst them asking how they had enjoyed the trip. They had enjoyed it, but were looking forward to being home to tell their adventures to their folk. They showed me some of the gifts they had bought for family. Not to be outdone, the youngest traveller opened his case. It was packed with every type of bottle he had managed to cram in ... 'For my Dad!'

If the Customs ...! Peterhead! Here I come!

During that trip, we had taken an excursion to vet a 'Colonie' layout near Le Touquet. It was run by the French Railways for the benefit of the children of its employees. It was possible for outside agencies to book its use when the SNCF were not using it.

We did try it and enjoyed a new-found freedom abroad. The daily timetable and routine was ours. We were handy to a beach and sea-water was distinctly warmer than back at home.

It struck me that we could try a little 'Colonie' experiment in Shetland, if only for a long weekend.

The school up-country in Voe seemed a likely spot. It was not a large community, fairly apart from the houses in the area. We were able to get thin polystyrene mattresses which unrolled to offer protection from a cold floor and comfort from bumps and hard parquet blocks. A group of senior girls, in the company of the charming French assistante, Mademoiselle Michèle Cabille, would camp out in the school, organising their own ploys and cooking for themselves.

The main object of the exercise, since they had a native French speaker, was for them to conduct the whole weekend in the 'parlez-vous'.

The Head and I took the small party and their gear out by car, saw the equipment unloaded and left them to it.

Since my own daughter was on the trip, I got some idea of the fun and games they had had. Perhaps not so much French had been spoken as we might have expected. There had been some annoyance from a handful of local youths; but, all in all, it had been a pleasant weekend. The weather had behaved itself. It had been a 'first' in Shetland, at least. I think a house at Voxter, owned by the Authority, was later used in the same way, but with other scholastic disciplines bringing students together. (See "French Weekend Camp" page 40).

One more language experiment was yet to be tried and it needed a Frenchman to carry it out. Jean Renaud came to the Institute with a degree in Norwegian from his home university in Caen, Normandy. He was interested in studying Norse matters and, in Shetland, Norn, the old language of the islands.

French and German were taught in the school. French was a must, apparently, because there was an RAF station in Unst, serviced by married men and their families. Like most service units, they were mobile, likely to be transferred to another station periodically. The children would best fit in to the English system if French was the foreign language they were taught in school.

I felt that, if there had been no RAF or similar foreign element in the islands, Norwegian would have been a more practical language to teach as a first foreign tongue.

Quite a lot of Shetland expressions are Norwegian in spelling or pronunciation. The War had strengthened the link between the two lands. Norwegians of 'The Shetland Bus' fame and others of their fellow-countrymen married Shetland girls, taking them back across the sea when the fighting was done. Many Shetlanders head on holiday to Norway. Lerwick is twinned with Måløy, a fishing-port like itself. There is a Norwegian seafarers' mission, staffed by a Norwegian and his family. Signs in shops and banks indicate that Norske penger are welcome in Shetland tills and bank vaults. Norwegian and Danish fishermen are regular callers in port.

Jean Renaud's presence was too good a chance to miss. I decided to discuss the possibility of submitting some pupils for the 'O' grade exam in Norwegian. Some of them would have great difficulty with French at that level, but Norwegian looked easier. It was always a chance of giving someone an opportunity to acquire an 'O' grade in a foreign language, and thence, a step up into post-secondary education at university or technical college.

Anywhere else than Shetland, Orkney or the Outer Isles, a fly would have been found in the ointment. Jean was not a qualified teacher and registered as such with the General Education Council, as behoved a professional teacher. The behoving was a requirement of fairly recent date.

The Head approved of my decision. About a dozen candidates came forward to try the innovation. A half-dozen gained a certificate. A Bressay girl, one of the Sutherland sisters, a younger one, if I remember, went on to graduate in Swedish at Aberdeen! Today, Norwegian flourishes.

A highly talented language colleague bears the torch. Derick Herning and I decided to try the Scottish 'O' grade and later, 'Highers' in Norwegian. We were successful, he more so than I. I passed, I fancy, because from experience of teaching languages to certificate level, I knew what the examiners were looking for, and, as I had advised pupils, I took my own advice and kept things simple but correct.

Often in teaching, particularly at secondary level, we have little idea of how successful our work has been. It still gives me quite a kick to think that I was in on the ground floor when schoolkids opted for Norwegian.

And what about Jean? We still exchange Christmas wishes. He gives me an up-date on his work in the Norse languages, in which he can list translations from various branches of the subject and learned theses, dissertations and publications. Mange takk.

Derick hit the headlines fairly recently, gaining the title of 'The Polyglot of Europe'. He outspoke other entrants with his grasp of more than a score of languages. He was most annoyed when certain interests wanted him to list various expressions for making progress with 'dolly-birds'!

FRENCH WEEKEND CAMP

DURING THE weekend of 16th-18th July 1967, a camp 'á la française' was held for girls from classes III to VI of the AEI in the Olnafirth School, Voe.

The idea was suggested by Mr J.H. Spence, Director of Education, himself keenly interested in Modern Languages, and was enthusiastically supported by Mr Rhind, Rector of the AEI, who assisted generously with transport. The staff of the Modern Languages department organised the details of the camp - menus, activities and transport.

After stoking up with a good tea at home, 11 of the party left Lerwick at 6 pm on Friday. One group with guitarist sang its way to Voe with such old favourites as *Alouette* and *Frère Jacques*. Friday evening was spent in settling in, with games and a sing-song, new French songs being added to the repertoire.

On Saturday, in glorious weather, the party, plus dog, set out round Voe and over Sneugie (240m) to Gonfirth, where they swam and sunbathed and had picnic meals. The return was on foot by the Gonfirth-Voe road. Five extra pupils had arrived at the camp after work on Saturday to join in the fun.

With another fine day on Sunday, the party hiked across to Laxo where they spent the day swimming and sunbathing. By 5 pm the first of the transports arrived. I was greeted by a hostile band who were not at all interested in going back home. It had been 'fab', 'fantastic', 'marvellous'. In their enthusiasm they forgot their efforts at French. One camper, however, had aquired a French nick-name - 'La Gourmande'!

Some effort had definitely been made to speak French; but, frustration at not being able to express themselves satisfactorily, had forced many into speak-ing English.

There is no doubt that the camp was a great success. The only thing that marred it was the intrusion of a few local 'galants', whose nocturnal behaviour was annoying, to put it mildly.

Our thanks are due not only to those already mentioned, but also to Mr Jim Peterson, County Youth Organiser, for help with camping gear, the staff and cook of Olnafirth School who so readily accepted us, and our chauffeurs who helped considerably with cars.

Finally, a special word of thanks to Mademoiselle Cabille and Miss Cowan, who devoted their weekend to their pupils.

'THE SOUND OF MUSIC'

THEY SAY (that nebulous 'they') that there is often a link between language and music. Musicians have the ear which lends itself to the acquisition of a foreign tongue! Does it work in the opposite direction? I think I know what the retort would be from my fellow-players in the Lerwick Brass Band!

Jimmy Dorrat had called across the street to me, suggesting I join the Band on the strength (unknown to the Band!) of my ability to play the clarinet. Really, the clarinet ought to have been my second instrument. My first should have been the piano. Mam was a qualified piano-teacher. It was all to hand for us children, there at home. Yet none of us took advantage of her talent.

I was introduced to the bandmaster, Drew Robertson, and invited to come round to a practice night on Tuesday. In a brass band the reediness of the clarinet does not accord. It is an acceptable instrument in a military band. Not having a spare cornet at the time, the Band suffered me and my reed.

There was one aspect of music I was really looking forward to. During my training year in France, I had been a tenor member of the 'Chorale' of Grenoble University. I couldn't read music to adjust my voice to the little blobs and fatter rings of the medieval tunes we sang. I just stood close to Jean or Julien, fellow students and neighbours on the corridor of the Lycée Champollion, and sang their tune! The effect of being amid the four-part volume of haunting sound was fantastic. Rarely, but still stirring the emotions, some of those tenor parts come back to me. In the Band I would find again an opportunity to enjoy those riches.

Gilbertson Park was the local sports stadium. The Band met on Tuesday evenings, in a room of the pavilion which also offered accommodation to football players. Drew's desk was at the front. He looked over it to chairs and music-stands arranged in arcs, filling the rest of the space. On his right was the cornet section with horns to the left. Behind sat the euphonium and baritone players. At the back came trombonists and the players of the heavy metal, double Bbs and Ebs and a youth on the 'tymps'.

Quite an age range was represented. There were some of my pupils from 1st year and others ranging up the school. The core consisted of lads in their late 20s to the early 40s. The doyen was Bobby Burgoyne, assistant bandmaster.

We were drawn from various careers, colleagues, teachers like myself, engineers, officials in local administration, professionals concerned with our physical health and members with commercial interests. We were tall, short, thin or stout, clean-shaven, bearded, a motley throng, whose diversity was better concealed under uniform.

'Uniform' almost had me drummed out of the Band. It came about through an early morning broadcast on the radio. Jack De Maneo was the anchor-man of the *Today* programme. It was June month, 1966. Merchant seamen were on strike. Merchant ships were our life-line. The bulk of our provisions, everyday household needs, construction materials and vehicles came by sea. On the mainland, these items were available by motor transport. The strike had less effect there on the mass of the nation.

At 7.30 on a Friday morning, Jack suggested that salads were a good buy for weekend meals. I was so incensed, that I rang up the BBC in London, advising them to cancel that part of Jack's broadcast at the end of the repeat programme at 8.30, at least for the Northern Isles. We had little prospect of anything in the way of tomatoes and fresh lettuces for the foreseeable future, due to the strike. It was asking too much; yet, a hint of apology could have been made.

That was not the end of the story. Our Band committee had been engaged in negotiations with a band in the south to buy their old uniform. The garments had been packed in two big cardboard cartons, the caps and jackets in one, the trousers in another.

The strike came to an end. Delivery of goods resumed. We eagerly awaited the new uniforms. Alas! Somehow, the cartons had become separated. Only the caps and jackets arrived. The breeks were still on Matthew's Quay in Aberdeen!

The comical side of this affair prompted me to drop Jack De Maneo a line. I gave the details of the lost attire and added that the shipping crisis had, at least, an amusing side to it.

Imagine my surprise, when Jack read the letter out on one of his morning programmes. I wasn't the only one who had heard it. At the next Band practice, on the notice-board, someone had pinned a cutting from the northern edition of *The People's Journal*. A copy of that cutting appears on the opposite page.

My style comes from Andy Stewart's humorous song about the wearing of the kilt!

I had been a member of the band barely a month, and here I was, evidently 'taking the mickey'. Band authority, from then on, was a bit wary of me, I fancy!

A year's programme would consist of Sundays at kirk when the Band played the hymns. Hymn-playing was a feature of parades on Armistice Day. Programmes were arranged for outdoor concerts, seldom shone on by a sun that would allow us to play in shirt-sleeve order. Indoor concerts were performed in the Garrison Theatre to full houses. There were also requests for special events, like the opening of the Sea-angling Festival competition. This was a colourful day, as the flags of all the competing nations flew from flagstaffs along the harbour front.

One event was unique. On the last Tuesday in January, whatever the weather, the band was on parade to play the music of the fire festival, Up-Helly-A'. The suite had been composed by a Lerwegian, Dr Manson, who had close ties with the Band from the days when he had been its musical director.

On practice night the week before the festival, the Guizer Jarl and the Committee visited the bandroom. In the Garrison Theatre, there had been rehearsals of all the guizers from all the squads who would be parading in the march, when they accompanied the galley, a replica longship, to the burning-site. The traditional songs would be sung: the Marching Song, the *Galley Song* and the *Norseman's Home*. The latter is still for me quite a moving tune, sung as the torches are thrown into the longship. The Viking tradition was for the dead chieftain to be laid in his boat, which was then cast off, aflame.

The Committee's visit was an excuse to have the Band play the songs, then for all present to ease parched throats in the enjoyment of a convivial evening.

When the moment came for us to leave Shetland, the Band threw a farewell party in the bandroom. Needless to say, a good time was had by all.

In Shetland Library there is a cine film I made of the Band members and some of our activities. Happy hours!

Lads, may you keep your teeth! Firm be your lips! 'Let's take it again from...!'

Strike up the (breeks-less) band !

To : The Editor, " People's Journal."

DEAR Sir,—Despite the seriousness of it (and we in Shetland are extremely angry about it!), the seamen's strike has its funny side.

Lerwick Brass Band is in a predicament.

Its new uniform was due before the strike. Two parcels were made up; one of blazers and the other of trousers.

The blazers got through on the last shipment!

Yours draughtily,
Donald " Where's-Your-Trousers?" Smith,
3rd Cornet,
82 King Harald Street,
Lerwick.

UP-HELLY-A'

THERE WAS one feature totally unique to Shetland. Moors, peat, dales and hills, sea, cliffs and strands, islands, wild birds, sheep, narrow roads, harbours, ships, fishing- boats, we'd come across all of these before we had ever set foot in the Northland.

We knew of Spring rites, the bathing in the dew on May Day morning, fire festivals at mid-summer, Halloween and 'dookin' for apples', Guy Fawkes, and firework displays for the 14th July to honour 'Bastille Day' in France, which make so many of our civic attempts at pyrotechnical shows look like the proverbial damp squib!

Up-Helly-A' was and is in a class of its own. In my first draft of this account, I had made slight mention of it and the part which the Brass Band played in the event. My eldest daughter was critical.

"You'd need to give more detail for the general reader. What you have written leaves the outsider wondering what the terms means."

When the last Tuesday in January was approaching, it was soon explained to me by my colleagues. They were already organised into a squad, the teachers' squad. First and foremost, it is very much a male event. The female of the species is gulled into all kinds of supporting ploys, where skills such as needlecraft and baking are required. Without their womenfolk, the guizers would be hard put to it to make the festival what it is.

So, we've got guizers. As the name implies, disguise is the basis of their act. A squad is a group of men, of lesser or greater numbers, who stay together in a life-long unit to play their part in the festival. Play is used in the dramatic sense of play-acting.

A squad chooses to parody a topical event, local, national or international. They decide on a title and submit their idea to the Committee. If that idea has already been accepted, they must come up with a different one. Examples may clarify the situation.

There had been reports in the national press of several prison break-outs. One squad came up with an acronym: L.G.T.H.O.O.H. (Let's get the hell out of here!) For props, they had hardboard sheets painted to represent the walls and gateway of a prison. Most of the squad were in prison garb, loose smocks decorated with broad arrows. Some of them carried rope-ladders, whilst others in warders' uniforms ushered them in through the gateway.

In the official situation, Earl Mountbatten had been appointed to inspect the prisons in the company of a couple of civil servants. Two of the squad wore pinstripes. The Earl was in naval uniform. All three were masked. They were perfect look-alikes for, in Shetland, the moulding of face-masks had been tuned to a fine art.

The regulation squad musicians were on hand, the fiddlebox-carrier and an accordionist. As they played *Show me the way to go home*, prisoners could be seen throwing their rope-ladders over the prison walls, attempting a successful break-out.

A local take-off concerned the Guizer Jarl. This year he was the chief official in the Health Office. One squad dubbed themselves 'The Water-loo Vikings'. They appeared in towelling, babies' potties as helmets on their heads, toilet-seat tops acting as shields and lavatory-pan brushes were their swords. They displayed a device, painted on a large sheet of Izal toilet-paper, which read:

'WE AIM TO PLEASE' — 'YOU AIM, TOO, PLEASE!' (beneath a sketch of a misdirected 'penny-being-spent'!)

The Guizer Jarl is the head of the whole event. The Jarl's Squad always mans the longboat. Its members are drawn from close male relatives of the Jarl. Theirs is always a striking Viking-style uniform — winged helmet, sheepskin doublet and leggings, cross-banded with leather thongs as leg-dressings. A fearsome axe completes the ensemble. They are truly an imposing sight.

As for the longboat, until recent times, its construction was kept highly secret. So much interest is being shown now by tourists, that the building-shed is thrown open in the season, so that folk, who may never attend the winter festival, can gain some idea of the tradition.

The skills of a shipwright are needed. This is no job for enthusiastic novices. Clinker-planked down to what would be the water-line, she is a magnificent replica of the Viking longships of old. Her boat base, keel and so on, is replaced by a flooring, so that she can be trundled out on a bogie for her exhibition down at the harbour, then later, when she is paraded at the head of the whole procession to the moment of her burning. During this moving final spectacle, care was taken to rescue the proud, bearded figurehead for use in her successor, although this is now no longer the case.

Another feature of the event is the posting of The Bill. This is a proclamation set up at the Market Cross. It demands a high level of artistry both with paints, brushes and words, for it pokes fun at various worthies and public figures, outlining their misdemeanours, sometimes less well known to the general public, say, during a local councillor's time of office. It is all very much in the strain of 'no holds barred'!

For me, one item remains unforgettable. It concerned the Harbour Master of the time, Capt. Willie Inkster. In the year of the festival he had been honoured by the Queen with an OBE. This decoration appeared on The Bill with the addendum — 'For Ordering Boats Everywhere'!

The great day begins with the hauling of the longship from its shed down to the harbour in the centre of the town frontage. The Brass Band is on parade, leading the procession. The Guizer Jarl's Squad pays visits to the schools, hospitals and Old Folks' Homes. They pose in their longship for a photo call.

Excitement is shared by the younger generation, for they have their own longship and the accompanying ceremonies. Their Guizer Jarl is related to his senior. Under the guidance of Junior School technical staff, the building of their longship has been a project of the school term.

The junior guizers (Jarl's and classmate squads) set the evening festivities going. At 5.30pm on the Town Hall clock, they march into the burning-site, singing the traditional songs and proudly bearing their torches, brightly blazing in the utter darkness of a winter's night in these northern latitudes. They circle the longship at the right moment, hurl the flaming brands into the heart of the vessel. The intensity of the blaze gives sufficient light for even a simple cine-camera to record the glowing faces and historic costumes.

We were lucky. Our house was only a hundred yards away from the incident, as it takes place in the adjacent children's play-park. This offered a wonderful spot for filming — the children's chute. From it, I had quite an aerial view of the proceedings. There was still time left for these guizers and spectators to return home for tea, before the real action began. In this interval, the senior squads were making their way to Hillhead, coming together from all parts of the town and forming up into their squad positions. I knew of as many as 800 men participating in the event.

The moment arrived. The longship was towed between the ranks of all the guizers to take her place at the head of them all. At 7.30pm precisely, a maroon was fired. At its booming and flare, from each squad, a guizer rushed to the firing-point to gather the igniting-flame for the torches of the rest of his mates.

Suddenly, the whole street at Hillhead was glowing in a reddish fire as torches received the flame. The torches are quite a burden, being a cylindrical mass of sacking and burning-material, soaked in paraffin at the end of a stout carrying-stake of 2x2 wood, probably some five feet long. They must burn for a good two hours, throughout all the parading to the final burning.

A colleague told me it could be quite a dicey experience, especially on a blustery night. As they march with torches born aloft, red-hot ash drops from the sacking. If it finds its way inside an opening in a guizer's tunic, there is little he can do about it, except grin and bear it! That risk is ever-present!

All the time, the Brass Band was blasting forth, leading the guizers who were singing the traditional songs. The Up-Helly-A' song enlivened the marching, as the procession came down from Hillhead into King Harald Street.

This is a wide thoroughfare, so wide that the guizers can march and countermarch in four lines. The facades of the houses on each side of the street were aglow in the yellow gleam of the paraffin-fed torches.

Eventually, the parade turned into the burning-site. The galley was placed upon her stand. The Jarl and his men took their places round about. The rest of the guizers circled round behind, taking up position, until everyone was in place. The group would be some six-deep, torches held aloft.

The Band stood in its corner. To the words of the *Norseman's Home* , guizers sang the haunting tune. Then the bugle-call rang out.

This was the signal we had all been waiting for. With military precision, the torches were hurled into the heart of the galley. It must have taken some effort to fling the ones from the back row. Their trajectory had to ensure a safe, though no doubt, hot passage above the heads of the other throwers.

Instantly, flames leapt into the air. I learned later that a quick and successful burning was assured by gallons of paraffin stored underneath the longship!

As we joined in the singing of *The Galley Song* every eye was following the progress of the blaze. Up and up rose the yellow tongues of fire.

'There goes the mast!' went the cry. The Raven Banner no longer fluttered menacingly.

The heat was so terrific that the beard of the figurehead was beginning to singe. It was time to be on hand for its rescue. Gradually, the fire died down. Folk began to move away; yet the night was just beginning!

What was to follow was a long night of theatricals, feasting and dancing. Throughout the town, a dozen centres were open, school gyms, hotel ballrooms, even the vast but somewhat cooler space of the auction mart! Each venue had its hosts. It was at their invitation only that we, the general public, could gain admission. I think there was no restriction at the mart.

This is the point where the ladies of the community made their mark. They emerged from the background to feed us all and partner the males in the dancing. The culinary preparations had been going on for weeks beforehand. That was very much needed, since guests and guizers would be eating and drinking until breakfast-time at least, as the routine progressed.

Soup, sandwiches, reestit mutton, cakes and sweet dishes graced the menu. Most items were available all through the night. Space was set aside for dining.

On a platform the resident band played the usual medley of dance-tunes and the request items asked for by each squad. The dance-floor was surrounded by the abandoned female population, the young, very young, the older generation and the disabled. I should never have been able to keep up with the marching; but I did my valiant best on the dance-floor.

The custom was for a squad to enter and perform their piece in the middle of the hall. Mostly they provoked much hilarity. Many of the ladies who had had a hand in some brief fashioning of an item, must have been astonished at what the finished article revealed. The teachers' squad had kitted themselves out as Japanese Samurai. They wore glittering flowing robes and carried impressive swords. What these lacked in martial display, was redeemed in a clever sword-dance routine.

Once the act was over, the squad broke up and joined in the dancing. They passed up their request to the bandleader and picked out their partners for the dance. For a brief moment, a couple would enjoy each other's company, then he was gone and she remained to make the best of the rest of the night.

We had received an invitation to the Bell's Brae School hall. There they had a feature which may have been common to all the halls. It was a board on which they recorded the entry of each squad. In this way, we could see how many more were to come.

The movement of the guizers through the halls demanded a precision and organisation which a military commander might have admired. The troops were expected to behave themselves impeccably. No doubt, they partook of some refreshment stronger than lemonade to keep them going on their arduous round. Nevertheless, the rule was strict: anybody stepping out of line and behaving in a drunken manner was banned from taking part in the festival for evermore!

I think we wended our way home early enough to snatch an hour in bed before breakfast. In some halls the last of the revellers were still performing.

Two things are impressed on my mind. Lerwick must be the only capital which is entirely closed down for a whole day, for nobody stirred as far as I can recall. Secondly, we noticed a subtle difference in the extension of daylight from then on. It was as if the Up-Helly-A' torches had signalled to the sun that it was time to get a move on!

GOING! GOING! ...

AN ADVERT had appeared in *The Shetland Times* announcing a sale at Harry Hay's auction rooms. We were quite used to auction rooms in Dundee, Marshall & Johnston's, Ben Fenton's and Curr & Dewar's. There we had furnished a bedroom. My in-laws had provided an old-style, but tasteful dining-suite as their wedding-gift to us. My successful bids were limited to rusty woodworking tools and garden implements. Some are still in use forty years on.

We had been wandering along the Street. At the Market Cross we turned into Mounthooly Street and made our way up. It wasn't long before we saw by the oddments lying around that we were at Harry Hay's. A broad, wooden, outside stair led up to a wide doorway. I learned that the auction room had been a sail-loft in the old days. That would explain its vastness. Before the advent of the steam-driven engine, boats of the fishing-fleets had relied on sails and oars. Acreages of canvas were needed.

We nudged our way along with the throng of folk, who were familiar with the layout of the dingy atmosphere. Through a wide doorway, the saleroom opened out before us. At first glance, it was typical of auction rooms. Tables displayed smaller items, crockery, cutlery, ornaments, jewellery and bric-à-brac.

The main concourse was lined with chairs, lounge-, dining- and easy-chairs. Large pieces of furniture, tables, wardrobes and the like, as if to keep out the non-bidders, acted almost like a rampart, surrounding the arena, where a relatively quiet battle would be fought, the vociferous thrusts of the auctioneer being parried with a silent nod, a wink or a twitch of a finger.

Yet despite the similarities, this auction room was different in one respect. The two front rows of easy-chairs were already commandeered by a regular band, not quite Amazons, but formidable Shetland womenfolk, armed with wires and girded round with a leather belt, which at a certain point bulged into a padded ellipse. This leather device was pock-marked with holes, where a wire could be conveniently sheathed out of harm's way. We were to learn that this was the traditional knitting-belt of the islands.

It was Joe Laurenson who had first baffled my wife with the expression, wires. He had been commenting on the knitting ability of our bairns. They were busy with their knitting-pins.

The auction began. Harry was a good representative of his brotherhood. He had the patter and the jocularity, knew many of the bidders, but, how he ever saw the bids made in the front rows, beats me. The fingers twitched and twirled the soft Shetland wool into the complicated Fair Isle patterns.

One might have been excused thinking that the occupants of the front rows had merely come along to enjoy the shelter and the company. I could see no sign of any of them being interested in the going-ons just beyond their wires; yet, "to Mrs R ..." and the item was knocked down to one of the knitters! They carried on, even when the chairs they occupied went to someone in the crowd round about.

As I think back to it, the scene was worthy of a Pieter Breughel, the Elder. The northern features were not so unlike those of the Flemish village folk of his paintings. Faces tanned by the weather, features lined with age or care, worthy folk who knew toil and trouble, all were there; and mixed in the throng, mischievous youth squirming about, roundish shapes for the most part, clad as they were in the bulky wrappings of anoraks, scarves and fishermen's navy-blue jerseys.

It was a different scene at the cattle mart, where we discovered we could bid for a Shetland lamb. It was too much for my wife to see these pathetic, tiny creatures bid for and then led away to their doom. Stripped of their fleece, which was a valuable part of the trade, they seemed little bigger than a well-fed hare. The flavour of their meat was something different altogether, a delicacy we enjoyed down to the last bite. The fleece made a comfortable bedside rug on the chill lino.

THE 'AULD ROCK' WITH MANY GEM-STONES

PERHAPS one of the simplest mistakes a visitor to Shetland makes is to misjudge the size of the archipelago. There is the North and South Mainland, held together by a thread of land at Mavis Grind, which separates the Atlantic on the west from the North Sea on the right, penetrating deep into the land mass via Sullom Voe.

Far to the west rises the 'End of the World', Foula. To the east, the limit might be marked by the Out Skerries. Unst is the northern isle, whilst Fair Isle is the southern outpost.

Coming up the east coast from Sumburgh, one can readily identify Mousa by its broch. Across the sound from Lerwick lies Bressay, watched over by The Ward and its TV mast. Just beyond Bressay, the small island of Noss is, at one point, probably the noisiest spot in Shetland. Its cliffs house myriad seabirds. Whalsay lies between Bressay and the Out Skerries.

The link between Lerwick and the RAF on Unst is forged by a series of ferries and the intervening island of Yell. Fetlar is aloof just to the east, midway up the Yell coast.

Coming left about as we head back south down the west side of the Mainland, we note Papa Stour in St Magnus Bay. Papa Little hugging the coast gives a clue to the meaning of 'stour' in its sister's name. Stour is from the Norwegian for 'big'. In the same bay, but linked to the Mainland shore by a bridge from the road to Brae, is Muckle Roe.

The southern coast of the bay is the shoreline of the mass of the west side of the Mainland, an area pock-marked with peaty lochs and fringed in tatters of voes and firths. Off its southern shore lies romantic Vaila.

A chain of islands close in to the backbone of the Mainland may no longer be termed islands. Where, in the 1970s, a ferry linked Scalloway to Hamnavoe on Burra Isle, bridges on Trondra have now turned the self-sufficient community into a complex of commuters from Lerwick who have built some luxurious dwellings on prime sites.

Below Burra and halfway to the cliffs of Fitful Head, St Ninian's Isle plays, according to the state of the tide, a coquettish game of 'Tease' with the mainland, as its sandy ayre, a natural causeway, is engulfed by the water rising on both sides on the golden link.

In three and a half years on Shetland, of all of these islands, I only spent hours ashore on Mousa, Bressay, Noss, Unst, Burra and St Ninian's. I had time to stretch my legs on Whalsay as the 'North' boat discharged cargo. We were heading on a trip to Unst. The rest were so near and yet so far!

The islands we did visit hold special memories. Bressay, the nearest, was reached by a regular ferry from Lerwick harbour. In calm weather, the crossing of Bressay Sound is a delightful trip; but, I've watched from my classroom window, heart in mouth, as the boat fought its way across from Bressay in the teeth of a south-westerly gale.

Most visitors used Bressay simply as a stepping-stone to Noss and the seabird colony. A narrow channel is all that keeps the keen birdwatchers from their goal. The boatman, who runs a croft on Bressay and pastures sheep on Noss is the contact for the crossing.

We did the trip at the height of the nesting-season. Friends had warned us. We had to cross the territory of the Bonxie as the Arctic Skua is known to Shetlanders.

"Watch out for the parent birds diving at you!" they said.

There was little wonder. The baby birds were a darkish-grey, lost amongst the tufts of grass. As we were keeping a lookout for them, the parents showed their displeasure at our intrusion by diving dangerously close to our heads. The best protection was a stick held aloft.

Bill Chaloner, our holiday guest, had a bright idea. We had eaten our picnic which had been packed in a tall, stout brown-paper shopping-bag. He pulled it onto his head and walked blithely amongst the birds, oblivious of their attacks!

Baby Bonxies lay cowering in the grass. We picked them up gently, curious to see them at closer quarters. Carefully they were returned to their bed. Parents dived and screeched about us.

The immediacy of the gull colony on the cliffs was signalled to us by the stench! Next moment, we were gazing over the edge at all manner of seabirds: Fulmars, Herring Gulls, Gannets or Solan Geese, Guillemots, Razorbills, Shags and Cormorants. Tystie, Scarf, Tammie Nories, intriguing Shetland names from the Old Norse.Which fits which of the above list?

The Tammie Nories were closest, hiding in burrows at our feet. They are the comical wee birds known to us as Puffins or sea-parrots, because of their bills. They fly with a frenetic beating of wings. When feeding young, they return from the rich feeding-ground of the Shetland sea, beaks festooned with sand-eels, like miniature portly bambinos, who have vainly tried to accommodate their first helping of spaghetti!

The wonder of the colony lies in the siting of an egg. A mere dimple in the rocky ledge suffices. The very ovoid shape of the shell is insurance against a crash onto rocks below. And the wonder is compounded by a bird's uncanny skill in finding its way back to the nest. It would seem easier to reach the flat of Mr Foo Chow in the high-rise blocks of Hong Kong!

And all the time, birds are plunging below the waves. A shag disappears. Minutes tick past. Then, suddenly a scrawny neck pops up yards away from the plunge.

Stonily set on a slab of rock, the purply-black bird is silhouetted against the sunlit sea, a sinister form, at least to its scaly meal below the surface, unaware of its fate.

Gannets fold their wings suddenly in flight. A sharp nose-dive from the height and they become a fish-spear, unerringly aimed. Does the golden crown and neckband dazzle the victim? Cruel is the head with bright blue eye and blue, sharp beak, set starkly against the glistening white body plumage. I am glad I am human and not whitebait.

Back on Bressay, we decided to go to the top of The Ward. To avoid the long trudge uphill, we hired a local Land Rover. Bairns and grown-ups, we all piled aboard. There is a road of sorts, because access is needed to the TV mast when maintenance is carried out by BBC engineers.

Stowed away at the rear, I had the impression at times, that all we needed was a booster rocket to thrust us into orbit, so steep was the angle of the bonnet of our taxi.

Our expectations for the view were in no way disappointed. On our right, the southern Mainland stretched towards Sumburgh. Below us across the Sound, sprawled Lerwick. The leftward arc encompassed the vast sea-scape, where, beyond the horizon, lay Denmark, West Germany, Holland, Belgium and France. Towards the interior of the island itself, were sheltered basins of greenery. A colleague told me that grapes were produced under glass on one of the crofts, snuggling out of the wind.

We decided to return to the ferry downhill on foot. Unwisely! Only a day before, I had set about choosing a new pair of shoes. They had ribbed crêpe soles, ideal I thought for walking.

If we had stayed on the road, all might have passed off smoothly. We decided to take a short cut and head downhill over the grassy slope. The grass was damp enough for me to slip. Once before, on a damp slope on the steep, steep side of Ben Lomond, I had slipped, wearing plimsoles and a kilt. In those days I had two sound legs. The only discomfiture I felt was the soaking as I tobogganed over a very wet bog. This time, my one good leg did not save me. I twisted my other ankle.

The descent to the boat was very painful, as I tried to hobble along, supported by my wife. We made it. But our relief was almost short-lived. Aboard the ferry one of the girls had clambered up onto the cabin top. There was nothing for her to hold on to.

"Come on! Let's have you down from there!"

The walkway round the cabin was quite narrow, easy enough to keep to once little feet were set on it. But manoeuvring, padded in layers of warm clothing did not help the bairn. She could barely see where to set her feet. She dropped — a lurch sideways! But for the firm grip of the ferryman, she would have been over the side!

Mousa was another delightful excursion with the Chaloner family. We left from the little pier, probably the private landing-place of the Lord Lieutenant of Shetland, who lived close by in Sand Lodge. The ferryman left us on the shore of a little cove overlooked by the broch. He would call back to fetch us later in the afternoon. We had quite a few hours to explore the place.

The broch was our immediate goal. I was reminded of the cooling-towers of the ICI factory at home. 'King Kong's Milk-bottles' we called them, because of their shape, an elongated concave neck, just like the bottles Rena delivered the Co-op milk in!

We gazed up at the Pictish fortress-home. It is built of stone slabs, overlapping, crevices filled with smaller slabs. We were surprised that it was 'double-skinned'. A similar wall on the inside was cross-jointed to the outer wall with slabs which formed a stairway to the lookout rim at the top. A drystane dyker would admire its proportions and invisible linking.

Entry is the test for a limbo-dancer! The Picts were a smallish race. No doubt, they came in with less trouble than we did. But there was method in their system. Invaders would be at a disadvantage, doubled up like a clasp-knife. As each foreign head protruded from below the lintel, a sharp tap from a stone club would prevent further intrusion!

The lintel stones and stairs were immense. One wonders at the technique they employed to set the slabs in place. At ground level, it would be relatively easy. How did they lift them into place as they built higher and higher?

The beaten earth floor was spacious. Round the inner wall, 'cupboards' were built for the storage of provisions and equipment. Rooms also were similarly fashioned. A fire could be set in the middle of the space. Probably, the whole building was roofed with branches and heather.

Bill Chaloner and others scrambled up the inner stair to the top. The view was extensive; but, hilly ground to the east offered some protection from the cruel wind that blows from that airt.

A surprise awaited us outside the Broch. As we walked over the grey stone slabs of rock, we could hear a cheeping. No birds were to be seen on the grass about us. The twittering was coming from beneath our feet! We learned that it was 'Mother Carey's chickens'. During daylight the Stormy Petrel shelters under the stone, to come out and go to sea in the dark! In such a small space on the island, we had met with all these wonderful new discoveries.

More awaited us beyond, as we set out towards the southern tip and then to the east. Lord Lieutenant Robert Bruce kept his thoroughbred Shetland ponies on Mousa. They were enjoying the freedom of the island as we strolled past across the southern tip. We turned and headed up the east coast.

Suddenly, we came upon a lagoon or almost one, so close was the lochan to the sea. At high tide the salt water would flow into it through a stony channel. Bald grey heads showing just above the surface were turned towards us. A band of seals were disporting in the pool.

Reports that seals were attracted by music prompted us to put the theory to the test. We tried them with the *Eriskay Love Lilt*, the haunting Gaelic song of a western isle. Amazingly, the seals turned and swam towards us!

We would try another contact, more direct. It was a sunny day. The lagoon was in a hollow sheltered from the breeze. How would the seals react if we swam amongst them? Rather warily, we slipped into the pool. It wasn't deep. The water was pleasantly warm. The seals didn't retreat. They seemed to have accepted us as other aquatic creatures. Perhaps, they were waiting for an encore.

Some decided to make for the open sea. In the short distance they had to travel, they showed not only awkwardness, but their agility. The outflow was a mere trickle at this stage of the tide, just enough to trace the route they had to follow. What an ungainly lumbering of burly, sleek forms! Then ... an explosive plunge and swish! They had reached the sea. In a flash, they were away!

This excursion was particularly exciting for our French friends from the Vosges. They had never been so close to creatures which they probably had not seen before. Their excitement was evident. We made our way back to the landing-stage for the ferry back home. French tongues jabbered away as they recalled the unexpected meeting.

The prospect of a weekend break on Unst lured us onto the North Boat, the *Earl of Zetland*, or the *Earl*, as it was commonly termed.

In 1958 we had been as far north as Toft on the Mainland, where we looked across the nine-knot tide of Yell Sound to the island of the same name. The quickest and most direct route to Unst is by road; but, the trans-island road on Yell needs the ferry links at each end to complete the run to Uyeasound. As I study the map now, I am intrigued by the route that the road takes across Yell, and later, on Unst, up to Baltasound, which was our destination on the boat.

I have never posed the question, but, I feel that the local folk would tend to take the overland route. The boat was probably more of a tourist attraction and a lifeline to the island communities, as it transported more easily the bulky necessities of life to the islanders and exported their farm produce, especially their cattle, sheep and ponies. Now, inter-island car ferries connect the North Isles.

From the moment of casting off in Lerwick Harbour, the journey was an adventure. Calm weather was a bonus. We passed through the North Mooth, as we made our way out to Whalsay and Symbister, the port of call. I did little more than stretch my legs ashore, whilst unloading and loading took place at the quayside.

Back on board we skirted the Lunna peninsula. It was to have special memories for us. For Shetlanders and Norwegians, memories are haunted by the daring deeds and tragedies of the Second World War. Lunna was the staging-post for members of the Norwegian Underground movement. Tiny fishing boats dodged the surveillance of the occupying Nazis, to take freedom fighters out of Norway or to return patriots, trained in the skills of saboteurs and undercover agents. Their story is told in *The Shetland Bus*, a gripping account of a nation's fight against the hated foe.

We headed for Mid Yell. I have a vague memory of a sandy bay. Midway up the hill from the shore stood a modern school building. I think we dropped anchor for goods to be unloaded and Yell products to come aboard.

Fetlar lies just off Mid Yell Voe. We were to see more of it on our homeward journey. Now, we were heading for Uyeasound at the southern end of Unst.

There is a ferry-boat pier in the harbour. The *Earl* with her dignified name did not deign to use it. Yet, goods and passengers had to go ashore. 'If the mountain won't come to Mohamet ...!' Mohamet appeared in the guise of a 'flit'-boat. To 'flit' is the guid Scots expression for to 'move house' and, in general, to 'transport'.

The flit-boat was an open motor launch, crewed by a pair of Unst 'Vikings', one, at least, was bearded, with a head of fair gingery hair, if I rightly recall.

The whole episode was enthralling to watch. When large oil-drums were lowered by the ship's derricks, I expected to see the cockleshell below turn turtle. The hold part of the launch was already pretty well packed with various shapes and sizes of cardboard cartons. Where would the drums be stowed? We should never have guessed! The only space left was a narrow ledge of planking running round the gunwales. The rubbing-strake offered an edge, high enough to stop the drums from rolling overboard into the briny. It was the delicacy of the handling which astounded me.

A toot on the ship's siren, a wave of the hand from the launch, full throttle and away she sped on a calm sea of the deepest and clearest blue. 'Chapeau!' to you, Unst mariners.

The 'ting' of the ship's telegraph and our engines came to life again, as we headed out northwards to Balta Sound. I have a very distinct picture in my mind

– 54 –

of the *Earl*, not a huge ship, as ships go, towering above the water, as she lay at anchor off Baltasound, the township, a cluster of houses round a hotel and a post-office.

The island north of 'Baltie' rises to the summit of Saxa Vord, which is just short of 1000 feet above sea-level. On the hilltop stands a listening-post, part of the chain which keeps 'tabs' on Soviet affairs. At the base is the RAF station which controls the outpost. What the present day situation is, I cannot say.

What I do record is the boast that the 'boys in blue' made.

"At mid-summer, we can play golf at midnight. You can read a newspaper without recourse to artificial light!" If we allow for the height, they are practically one degree closer to the Arctic Circle than we were on Mousa!

The northernmost tip of Unst is Herma Ness. The cliffs here are home to more large colonies of nesting seabirds. I never actually visited this precipitous cape, but I did become familiar with some of its inhabitants. On that occasion, I saw them working in their true environment, whilst I was far from being happy in mine — aboard a local herring-drifter, the *Venture* from Hamnavoe, Burra. Our crew was hauling in the nets in the dawn glow of an early summer day. The sky was alive with squawking gulls, seizing any chance to filch herring which fell from the mesh. It was a sight to see the Gannets diving down within feet of the boat. My stomach had got past the stage of being able to add to their breakfast diet!

Through conversation with my wife, I have discovered the reason for our Unst trip. We were not a complete family. Our eldest was still on mainland Scotland at a music camp in the Trossachs. Having no longer a 'pied-à-terre' in Scotland, we had decided to take this chance, with the other two girls, to see something of our new homeland.

We still have tangible evidence of the trip. Willie Peterson, an auctioneer in Lerwick, held a roup in the hotel where we stayed. One item was a wash-stand with a marble top. It was minus a towel-rail on the right hand side. The marble top was the big attraction. It would prove ideal for pastry-making! The item of furniture fell under the hammer to us for two shillings and sixpence (12 1/2p in today's money).

Really, we had saddled ourselves with something of a problem. Without the marble top, the cupboard section was not heavy. We didn't want to separate the two parts. The cupboard would be handy for baking-tins and the like. Friendly hands helped us to load the piece aboard the flit-boat, to warnings of: 'Mind our piece of Chippendale!' I think we ought to have paid portage on the *Earl*. We said nothing and no questions were asked.

Back in Lerwick, the wash-stand was offloaded. I fetched the car. In a matter of minutes the marble top and base were being set in the kitchen. It was ideal! The missing towel-rail allowed us to push the stand right up against the left hand side of the Aga stove. It did yeoman service for three years in No. 82 King Harald Street. In 1969, it said 'Goodbye' to its Shetland home and was moved with us into every house we've taken since!

On the way south from Balta Sound, we passed close to Fetlar. Brough Lodge, a chateau-like edifice where Lady Nicolson resided, made quite an impressive picture on the skyline.

How one reached the island then, I did not know, although the Shetland wildlife authority, Bobby Tulloch, had the answer. The snowy owl and otters are particular interests of his and are not strangers to the island now. The owl has only fairly recently, in this past generation, returned to Shetland. Bobby has kept tabs on it and its re-establishment. As mentioned previously the North Isles are connected by inter-island car ferries now.

Though my visit to Whalsay was only very brief, other members of the family took a trip across to visit the McRobbies of the Schoolhouse at Symbister. They took the ferry, a launch similar to the Bressay boat. The trip from Nesting was uneventful. Not so, the return.

During the visit, the weather had turned nasty. A strong wind had blown up, churning the sea in the channel into something bordering on a maelstrom. The cabin space of the little launch was packed. The bairns, seated on mother's knees, found themselves airborne on the crest of the waves, as the ferry plunged back into the trough. Never were travellers so happy, as when they finally struggled ashore. Mother had often wondered whether they would see dry land again! Local folk may not have been quite so concerned. They probably knew the boatman and had faith in his seamanship.

Of all the isles, St Ninian's was the easiest of access. We could drive down in the car to Bigton, park and walk to the island across the ayre. This sandy stretch was a source of seaborne treasures which delight bairns. They dawdled, searching right and left, calling to each other, 'Come and see what I've found!' Mother joined in the quest for shells and polished stones.

The island had hit the headlines when a local youth by the name of Coutts found a centuries-old silver chalice and plate in what had been a chapel. The archaeological site is now a place of pilgrimage for the visitor to Shetland, keen to see places of historical interest. Shetland wished to exhibit the St Ninian's Treasure in its own attractive museum, but Edinburgh was not at all willing to comply. The Treasure has enjoyed a brief stay on loan in the land where it belongs.

Like many other islands here, St Ninian's attracts its own quota of nesting sea-birds. Though the cliffs are not so high as on Noss, they offer plenty of ledge space for Fulmars to make their homes. It is an absorbing pastime to sit and watch their effortless flight, as they merely tilt their wings to the air currents flowing round the cliff face. Back and forth they wheel, hardly beating a pinion to continue their aerial ballet.

The view to the south is impressive, as the massive block of Fitful Head thrusts its greyness into the Atlantic swell. Its bulk may have helped to reduce the extent of the disaster caused by the wreck of the *Braer*. The southern slope of Fitful Head encloses the Bay of Quendale, where the helpless tanker was driven ashore by hurricane-force winds in January 1993.

There was no let-up in the storm. This prevented any attempt at salvage. The whole cargo of oil spewed out. A prohibited zone of 400 square miles at the southern end of the Shetland Mainland marks the area where fish and crustaceans are being polluted and their feeding-grounds as well. How long it will remain so, nobody can foresee.

Burra Isle had a special attraction for us, since I had made the acquaintance of the crew of a local fishing-boat. Jocelyn Laurenson was the daughter of Joe, a partner in the boat. As a senior pupil in the AEI, she was needing some advice about post-school prospects in teacher-training. I was able to help. So, I was introduced to Joe, Rachel and the family.

Like other island people, Burra folk are closely related. The *Venture* was skippered by Jim Cumming, Rachel's brother and Joe's brother-in-law. John, an older brother, and John James were all partners in the boat. With a warm invitation to visit them at Bridge End, we extended it to include some of our own friends who were exploring Shetland. Among them were my old French friend of Grenoble days, Henri Roche and an ex-Wren friend of my wife's.

We had to cross to Hamnavoe on Hance Smith's ferry from Scalloway. The seven or so miles from Lerwick to Scalloway were far from monotonous. On the main North road, we soon climbed out from the edge of the metropolis up to the masts of the Decca radio station. Behind and below was an extensive view of the town, its harbour, Bressay, the coast of Nesting beyond the Isles of Gletness (title of a haunting tune) and out to Whalsay.

Then came a steepish, winding descent to the Brig o' Fitch. Danger was compounded by the deep ravines cut in the peat by the rain-clouds. The presence of sheep with lambs separated from their mothers by the width of the road were a greater hazard. Without warning, a hungry lamb might make a dash for 'mother' across the way. Brakes squealed, bairns shrieked and drivers swore! We were told that 'on the mainland, folk drive on the left; on the continent, they drive on the right. In Shetland you drive down the MIDDLE!'

They tell the tale of the man who learned to drive on the five miles of road on the Out Skerries. He had to come to Lerwick to sit his driving test. He passed, then had his car loaded onto the *St Clair*. He was going on a touring holiday south.

On his return, friends asked how he got on with all the traffic. "Oh, that was no problem! There weren't any sheep!"

The other road to Scalloway led by the South Road and its turn-off just above Gulberwick. This part was quite narrow and twisty. It joined the Brig o' Fitch road just above the Scord. Here the route snaked down to Scalloway; but, there need be no haste. A halt at the top offered another marvellous view out to the west and south.

Out on the horizon, on a clear day, Foula seems temptingly close; yet, only the calmest of seas assures a safe landing on its cliff-girt shore.

Below, like an exploded jigsaw, islands and islets lie scattered amid the flow of Atlantic tides. What secrets do their names hide from the visiting stranger: Oxna, Burra, Trondra, Papa, Hildasay, Cheynies, Green Holm and Havra?

At the Scord, we are sitting on the spine of the south Mainland of Shetland. Homing on a trans-Atlantic flight aboard a Jumbo, I have thrilled to the breakfast-time sight of that slender land-form, as we flew down its length to an 'Au revoir' at Sumburgh Head. The Clift Hills, as the spine is named, are paralleled by Clift Sound whose deep waters wash the steep spine-side.

Scrutiny of a relief map only reveals a maximum height of less than 300m (1000 feet); but, and it is an imposing 'but', that topmost point rises directly from sea-level to add stature to what would be a mere pimple elsewhere!

On the Clift slope below the Scord, the Norwegian flag flew proudly at a white mast, above a white house. It was the home of Jack Moore, who owned a shipyard in Scalloway harbour. The flag was an everyday visible token of the gratitude of the Norwegian nation for Jack's services to the valiant freedom-fighters, who carried on a relentless campaign against the Nazi invaders. The efforts of Jack and his workers helped to keep The Shetland Bus to its erratic timetable. King Olaf of Norway personally decorated him for services rendered.

Close by the harbour, on a spit of land, stand the ruins of Scalloway Castle.

Its owners in centuries past held the island folk in tyrannical bondage, especially under Earl Patrick Stewart. Crossing to Burra on Hance's boat, we turned our backs upon its dreaded walls.

The novelty of the journey was heightened by the sight of islands all about us. Grassy holms fattened flocks of local sheep. Their owners put them ashore after the winter and herd them home at the end of the season, keeping an eye on their progress from time to time. Good grass cannot be wasted. On pebble beaches, without a human in sight, seals might lie basking in the sun.

From Hamnavoe, the harbour and ferry terminal, it was quite a trek across to Bridge End. The name is apt, because without the bridge, West and East Burra would stand apart.

On one trip, Henri Roche was delighted to spot some fungi in the sparse grass of the rocky island. He eagerly picked them, but none of us were prepared to share his interest. His was knowledge gained from his father who worked for the 'Eaux et Forêts' department of French administration in the High Alps.

Another trip to Burra ended with a private crossing in Joe's rowing-boat. He took us out from its mooring at Bridge End, down Lang and Stream Sounds, across the deep cleft of Clift Sound to West Voe by Wester Quarff. Disembarking was a rather damp manoeuvre, as there was no landing pier. Joe gallantly carried most of us ashore.

In earlier days, the track between Easter and Wester Quarff had been used to haul boats across on log rollers. The pass follows the 50m (150 feet) contour very closely, a distinct cut across the spine which reaches heights of 230m (700 feet) to 260m (800 feet) on each side of the pass. This haulage route avoided a long and dangerous sail round the tip of the 'Auld Rock'.

Island-hopping was naturally something of an adventure to us who had had the vastness of Highland Scotland to explore. Nevertheless, we began to miss the openness of the countryside around Dundee and its variety of exits. From Lerwick, one either took the North or the South road. These routes ran, for the most part, through a barren landscape of peat and heather, none so bleak as the Kames, that wind-battered wilderness between Sand Water and Voe to the north.

Yet, we all treasure memories, private or shared, of outings on the Shetland Mainland: bathing at Gulberwick or at the Sands of Sound, a Brownie camp in Weisdale and a visit to Shetland's forest close by, an educational survey of the superimposed relics of habitation at Jarlshof, from Pictish to 17th Century civilisation. More up-to-date exploration took us to the Point of Scattland, just a mile or two north of Lerwick, where wartime bunkers intrigued the bairns.

It was always possible to find a beach or burn where the enchantment of water kept the young ones happy for hours. At Vementry, out the West side, they had a good laugh at their dads, Joe and me, braving the chill waters of the voe on a so-called summer's day! I remember not so much Joe's walrus-like disportings, as the coldness of the briny!

Yet, it was so easy to go to the other extreme, and at a temperature of barely 18°C, find oneself severely sunburnt. There is always some movement of air in Shetland. Coming off the water, it tends to be cool.

We had found a sheltered corner in the hollow of a sand dune and prepared to do some sunbathing. The air was pleasantly warm. There was none of that stifling Mediterranean heat under which oiled bodies are basted to produce the trademark, 'Cooked on Foreign Strand'! So, unwittingly, we overdid it. We paid the penalty later and for days to follow, as lobster-pink skin peeled painfully off.

We had forgotten just how clear the atmosphere is over Shetland and for how much longer the summer sun in a clear sky shines intensely down. We never made the mistake a second time, not because the conditions were never again repeated. Once was enough to teach us the lesson!

There was another warning to be heeded. Shetland parents never failed to impress upon their bairns the danger of the banks. Nothing to do with credit cards; they were yet to be invented.

Banks are the cliffs, no matter how high. It is only too easy in that rocky land to go too close to the edge. Even a short fall might land the unwary on a nasty outcrop of boulders and jagged rocks. Unnoticed, an injured party could lie at the mercy of the tide and drown.

The same warning went for the harbour area. There is a steady current of movement along the quays. Fishing-boats unload. Men repair nets. Supplies are taken aboard. On occasion, one has the impression that the whole township is down to see the arrival or departure of the passenger-cum-cargo boats. Storms bring in flotillas of foreign fishing-boats. There was the regular appearance of the Soviet water-tankers. All this activity attracted its spectators.

In a careless moment, a slip could mean disaster. Crewmen paid the penalty of a missing footing, as they tried to guide unsteady drunken legs back to their floating home.

A tragedy occurred when a schoolboy, making his way between classes, wandered, unwilling student, down by the harbour instead of taking the more direct route to his class. He fell into the water. Rescue came too late.

We had our own moments when, at the very least, a false step could have meant a cold bath. This was on a cliff-side path leading to a spot of our most treasured memories.

It had all begun during the 1958 trip to Shetland on our visit to close relatives who were temporarily in exile. Brother-in-law had taken his sister-in-law to visit a crofting family who lived in the local parish. She had stepped back in time to a home where electricity was unknown in the house. She had walked on a floor of beaten earth and had sat under a roof of thatch. The matriarch, into her 90s, was cared for by a son and his two sisters.

I had been unable to go on the visit because my left leg, though strong enough after polio, was hampered by a calliper which was chafing on the side of my knee. That holiday saw the end of the pain. On our return to Dundee, I discarded the calliper and took to wearing boots for support of my ankle.

THE CROFT ON SWINING VOE

THE ACCOUNT of the visit was so vivid in my mind, that, now in Shetland, I was determined to make the trip. One fine Saturday afternoon in the summer, we set out for the croft. That visit and others subsequently inspired me to write my own experience of what I had so long wanted to do. Here is what I wrote:

At last! We breast the rise. Sharp, short, collie yapping. We've been spotted or smelt. A tallish figure stoops slightly out of the house. She waves. We wave back. Into the house she stoops again. Visitors spell hospitality.

From our vantage-point we can see the mouth of the voe. Its safe yet sinister presence of half a mile back is still on our right. At the tricky point on the cliff-side path, one false step by the unwary......slip......slither......then splosh! Not a sheer drop, but a steep grassy bank. I was never fond of cold baths!

The heather-clad moor rises from the water-line. It throws an embracing arm round the patch of green. The croft coories into it, snug from the wild sou'westers. Only the snell winds from an eastern airt can break through, for that way lies the long finger of rocky Lunna peninsula, an index pointing to the cold wastes beyond of the North Sea.

Relishing the tasty green amid the granite grittiness of the 'Auld Rock', the voe has taken a bite, a fair mouthful.

The tiny bay gives shelter to the boat, a Shetland model, which betrays its origins in sharp-pointed bow and stern. The wild sea-rovers of a thousand earlier years found haven in the voe. They stepped ashore, blond, blue-eyed, bearded wild men from the Northland, raven-winged-helmeted, proud conquerors of the foaming waters in their longships.

A wisp of blue smoke lazily curls from the chimney. Its ascent marks the unwonted calmness of the day. We trace it rising against the peaty moorland, losing track of it as the blue vault of the Simmer Dim gulps it up, licking cloud-lips savouring the peaty reek.

Our bairns tumble in joyous haste down the last slope, making a dash for the pebble beach, laughing and shouting, "Come and see what I've found!" Whorly-grained pebbles of russet, grey, white and purple are the treasure of childhood, jealously guarded and then forgotten, as some new acquisition enjoys ephemeral exclusiveness. We come down to their level more warily, yet our eyes reflect their happiness and light up with inward memories of days gone by.

A low dry-stane dyke marks the landward boundary of the bay. A little gate gives access to the haven. It turns in knacky smoothness, its hinge-post rotating in the green cup of an upturned wine-bottle. No sneck, just a twine loop, lassooing the latch post, holds it fast.

A few steps across the springy, close-cropped turf bring us to the open doorway. The sisters both come forward, lilting their welcome and pleasure at having visitors. Shy, head turned to one side, brother looks on indulgently at his happy sisters. We shall all meet face to face inside.

The bairns wait for no invitation to enter. They scramble through the doorway as if Ali Baba had given them his 'Open Sesame'. What riches are in store? Outside, we exchange greetings and enquire about each one's health since the last visit. We are ushered in, like the feathered flock into the hen-house at day's end. Hens share the entry with us, pecking at bits and pieces about the door. A wire-netting screen can keep them at bay, whilst the rare summer warmth enters the gloom. Yes, gloom, not depressing, but warm and snug, inviting, insulating. We stumble slightly. The floor knows no timber boards. Its dimpled surface hides beneath an expanse of congoleum, brightly patterned where the daylight from the doorway betrays its lively colours. The beaten earth tricks not only the legs of us humans, but the 'pins' of tables, chairs and stools. Familiarity has taught THEM to seek their balance on empty boot-polish tins, or knolls on the same contour-line.

A primaeval urge draws our eyes towards the hearth, the centre of home life till the square-eyed monster of this generation, beamed like a silvery Cyclops and threateningly, dared us to look elsewhere.

The hearth-stone lies level with the beaten earth of the floor. Peat blocks glow with a soft warmth, their blush hidden beneath a smooring of powdery white flakiness. Our nostrils twitch in the unaccustomed perfume of the peat reek. Peats won from the peat-bank open to the sky and song of lofty larks. No scrambling in coal dust and stygian pools of icy pit water, in the dark hell of a mine. No fierce blazing of that hard-won coal. A natural glowing gently eases its warmth into relaxing bodies, tired from the toil of working in the field, on the moor or out at sea.

The guests and the menfolk sit. The sisters bustle about hostess chores, chattering like magpies and stealing bits of the conversation in the passing. A tablecloth of a whiteness that Persil would give its softest suds for, covers the vast table from end to end. Then, the treasures of the potter's wheel are brought to light. The cutlery takes its turn. What secret combination unlocks the many-doored or rather, lidded hidey-hole of knives and forks and spoons?

A shelf runs round at cornice height. It is the cornice! We gaze upwards at a roof of thatch. A wee mouse on the cornice shelf, stops in its scurrying to gaze down on us! The shrill scream of bairns, not fearful, but excited by such a visitor in an unusual setting, frightens the tiny creature. It disappears among the thatch.

Shoe-boxes empty of their soles are taken down. Big sister takes out spoons. Back goes the box. Diametrically across the room, kid sister removes another box, labelled 'Clark's Start-rite'. Out rattle the forks. Back goes the box. The knives are tempted to duel with each other from yet another. My eye tries to solve the combination code. In vain!

Milk warm from the cow is served from a jug. Plates of cakes and buns are set out on the board. Home-made jams decorate their dishes in richly coloured naturalness. But, now is not the time to partake.

Our hostesses have kneaded bannocks. A griddle of 'U'-shaped rods is set above the peat fire. The dough is placed across the grid. We smell the goodness baking. We watch the floury dough sink closer to the glow, drooping through the loops. My mouth waters at the prospect of munching the browned furrow and its accompanying white ridges. Home-made butter will ease the bannocks' crispness across a discerning palate.

The griddle is removed. A kettle takes its place, hanging from a pot-hook. Soon, unbelievably so, it is singing its serenade to tea-time. The steaming water swamps the leaves. Beneath its cosy, the tea is masked.

All is now ready. A grace is said. We set to with a will. No gluttonous gobbling. There is time to converse, to joke and digest. What thoughts went through the bairns' minds as they listened to their elders, their own folk and these strangers of that northern land, glad to welcome them in? How vivid are their memories now, stirring in the depths of Alberta, Sussex and the Forest of Dean? Are we all ever linked telepathically when Shetland or Swining Voe is mentioned?

The meal over, we move back from the table. A soporific calmness settles over the gathering. For a while, we turn to our own thoughts. I gaze out of the only window of that room, a mere square less than a yard each side. Beyond its transparency lies the turf, the bay, the hillside of our approach and beyond, as if it were further off than the moon, London and all the wasted bustle of the metropolis and its sister cities. A peace that almost passes understanding comes over me. The moon looks down, a pale shadow of itself in that never-ending twilight of high summer in the North.

On the day when we set out on our first visit to the croft, we parked the car in the farmyard at the head of the voe. A walk of an hour and a half lay ahead. That is my time. We were quite surprised to see the farm lying in the shelter of a clump of trees, later identified as whitebeams. They were flourishing and quite tall, unlike the stunted, twisted sycamores, commonly striving to grow.

We passed through a gate into an open field. The voe edged it on our right. The ground rose gently ahead. I had to watch my step on the tussocky grass. Suddenly, my wife gave a shout, "Jean!" It was the younger of the two sisters. She was coming downhill towards us and she had an escort, or she was the escort! Over her shoulder was strung a pillow-case. It was to hold the supplies she was bringing back from the store in Vidlin, a good mile further on!

Her companion was a sheep! She had fastened a piece of twine round its neck. It was leading her along.

The last time the two ladies had met was eight years before. Now, twenty-seven years on, we are still in touch; but the croft is empty. Mother had died years before our visit. Teenie, the older sister, died after we left Shetland. Jean and Lawrie, her brother, had kept the place going until, one day, Jean was no longer able.

They are enjoying the rest of their days in a sheltered housing complex, on a slope in the village of Vidlin. From the window, they can look down on the community and the Vidlin Voe.

When asked, "What is your greatest pleasure?" Jean answers, "The electricity! I just have to touch a switch and there is light or heat!" Water is on tap, especially the hot. No more need to trim paraffin lamps or lay in a store of such fuel. Peats can still burn in the hearth, but the bannocks no longer droop through the bars above the peat embers. And cars go past the door! Lawrie is still the quiet man, listening to the weather forecast through a Norwegian radio station. "They give a truer forecast than the folk down in London!"

I suppose the croft and its kindly folk sum up what Shetland means to us — the heather hills, the peat-reek, the clear water of the voe, the unpolluted sky, the peace, the friendly 'crack' as news is exchanged, a slow rhythm more in tune with the environment and a hardy spirit born of the struggle to exist.

As I re-read this chapter, I become aware of the references to bathing and am reminded of an early 'recce' we did by the West side. It was early spring, not a particularly sunny day. There in the water by Olligarth, a huddle of youngsters in bathing-costumes were swithering to take the plunge. Their skin had a purplish hue! Then, on a distinctly inclement morning, down at the harbour, we watched the inter-island swimming sports. The sky was grey, as the drizzle swept in on an easterly breeze. The hardy competitors dived in and thrashed their way to the finish, the vigorous effort helping to stave off the icy chill. I shivered for them!

Yet, senior pupils spoke of the summer perk offered by the education department. There was quite some competition to be enlisted as a swimming-instructor in various communities throughout the island. Successful candidates could expect to spend hours in the briny encouraging their pupils.

For years there had been talk of a swimming-pool in Lerwick. We never saw it. It materialised just after our departure. Billy Dalziel, a fellow bandsman and GPO employee, landed the job as its first supervisor. He must have relished the change which took him indoors away from the elements of his postie's beat.

Does Gulberwick, along with the Sands of Sound and other beaches beckon the hardy to a refreshing dip?

A SHETLAND WEDDING

VIDLIN was to be the scene of an event to which we were invited through the kindness of my headmaster and his family relations. If my memory serves me right, it took place on 29th December, 1966. We were guests at a Shetland wedding! The art master, Bob Ollason was to marry Maisie Sutherland, who came from Vidlin. Bob was a nephew of our head.

The wedding ceremony took place in the tiny church of Lunna, on the peninsula of that name, which is washed on its west side by the water of Lunna Voe, an inlet of the larger Swining Voe. The Morrison's Croft at Sandwick, Swining lay almost directly west of the kirk.

During our 1958 visit, brother-in-law had taken us to see the remote little kirk. Parishioners in the upper gallery could have leant over and shaken hands with their minister, as he stood in the pulpit! We were shown 'leper-holes', where, in former times, food had been left by members of the congregation inside the building, for the sick leper members of the parish to collect on the outside, so that no contact was made to spread the disease. As a child, I had always thought that leprosy was a terrible disease associated with hot countries in Africa or places like India.

How we all crowded into the church for the wedding, I cannot remember. Yet, our departure is as vivid in my memory as if I was still at the scene.

Mid-winter was barely past. The days were at their shortest; so that, by the time we set off back for Vidlin, round about five o'clock, there was no light in the sky. Guests had arrived by car, having come from all over the Mainland. Headlights were switched on. Away they drove.

For some reason we were among the last to leave. We rounded a hill above Lunna Voe. Ahead, like red spots on the skin of a serpent, the tail-lights of the procession pinpointed the road we had to follow. They warned of danger at sections where the narrow track came perilously close to a plunge into Vidlin Voe.

Outside the village hall, drivers parked their cars on the area round about. We emerged from the winter dark into the brightly lit hall. Ushers were at the door of the hall, ready to show us into our places. A row of benches stretched down to the bottom of the hall alongside an equally long row of tables. Then came two rows of benches. There was no room for a passageway between. The whole pattern was repeated till the hall was chock-a-block.

The tables were already set with cutlery and crockery. The cold meats lay in slices on the guests' plates. Cakes and sweetmeats were set out down the centre of the tables. Once we were seated, there was no ready means of exit. The whole arrangement was necessary to accommodate us all.

The elders of the community had seen to the preparation of the delicate meat of the local sheep. The cooks' assistants brought in the steaming tureens of vegetables which were passed on down the tables until everybody had sufficient within reach. It was an appetising meal which we enjoyed in happy company.

At the end of this, to us, unique 'wedding-breakfast', we moved away from the tables. The assistants cleared the decks. The able-bodied among us gave a hand to set benches and chairs round the walls, leaving the main hall space for the dancing which was to follow. There was no special haste. Distant relatives had another chance for a bit 'crack'. Friendships of long date were renewed. There was a delightful family feel about the whole affair. We, outsiders, were brought into the family embrace. It was especially heart-warming to be greeting our old friends of the croft.

The band struck up, fiddle, accordion, drums. Couples took to the floor for traditional Shetland reels, Scottish country-dances, waltzes and one or two modern steps.

It is 'droothy' pleasure dancing the light fantastic. Refreshment was on hand, brought in on trays. Rows and rows of drams were passed round, yet, though the dancing went on well into the next morning, I never saw one guest the worse for wear. They simply sweated the alcohol out!

We left early, at the back of two o'clock in the morning! I think they were dancing at 5am! The bride and groom were still there with their guests!

On another occasion we attended the wedding of Jocelyn Laurenson and her groom, Brian Smith. Joe had been responsible for the festive arrangements. So it was, that on the day after the celebration, most of us turned up again to tidy up the local hall. Once the work was done, it seemed only natural to end the day with more dancing. Joe played for us on his accordion. I can well understand how folk who gather on the outer islands carry the festivities on for a week. It may well be many a year before they have a chance to meet up again with kith and kin in such merry circumstances.

Merriment, though, must, at some point, give way to gloom. We were to experience the sadness of a funeral party, not of direct family, but of an elderly neighbour. After the service in the kirk, only the menfolk accompanied the coffin to the kirkyard. Up among the wind-swept tombstones on the Knab, we stood bare-headed as the coffin was lowered into the grave. The greyness of the sky, reflected in the leaden waters of the Sound, only added to the heaviness of heart of close relatives and friends.

We also learnt of another Shetland tradition linked with death. If a widow was left in dire straits and had to sell off some of the family possessions, folk present at the roup, tended to bid over the odds rather than seek to profit from a neighbour's misfortune. In such ways, the community supported its needy members.

AT THE HERRING FISHING

IN THE Shetland year, tragedy was never far off. Fishing was a life of danger. Danger lurked in equipment on board, in a false step on a heaving deck, as hawsers and ropes wound in. Propellers fouled by lines astern could leave a vessel drifting onto a rocky coast. Fog suddenly coming down, storms unexpectedly breaking were hazards to be faced with calm. One can never know the anxiety of those waiting back at home, listening intently to the marine band wavelength, crackling the voices of their menfolk.

The blue of a summer sky and the flatness of the sea in the Bressay Sound tempted me, one Friday evening, to ask Jim Cumming if I might go with them on the *Venture* to a night at the herring fishing. I wanted to record the trip with my cine-camera.

We sailed south at about five o'clock. Despite the sun, the air over the water, as the boat headed south, was quite nippy. I had been warned to be well wrapped up. A whole fleet of local boats was on the move with us. John James pointed out the veteran of the fleet, the *Research*, a 'Zulu', so named, as they were built on the north-east coast at the time of the Zulu Wars towards the end of the 19th century. They had a markedly raked stern.

I sought the warmth of the wheelhouse, where Jim pointed out the equipment at his disposal. By taking signals from the Decca station, he would be able to pinpoint, for future reference, a spot where he had run into a shoal of the 'silver darlings'. There was also an 'Azdic'-type of machine, giving soundings which he could interpret as shoals of fish. "In the old days," he said, "they could tell where the herring were by the colour of the water or from the presence of seabirds. All that knowledge is gone today. Now, we rely instead, on the wonders of modern science."

Out past The Ward we were in the open sea. I began to feel a different motion underfoot, not to my liking! Toilet facilities were simply a bucket, aft, behind the engine-room cover. I was out of sight among coils of rope and odd bits of gear. It wasn't long before I was horribly seasick!

Normally, there is just enough bunk space for the crew. Since each man would take his turn on watch, there would be one bunk empty. Joe told me to take over his bunk. He would take the place left by his successor on watch.

At other times when I am at sea, I feel less ill generally when I am flat on my back; but, the atmosphere below deck was not at all conducive to an easing of my qualms. The heavy smell of diesel vapour was compounded by an all-pervading stench of oily herring! I don't suppose the lads themselves were readily aware of the smell, anymore than we had been on our Tay-Clyde cruise in 1954, aboard the *Joan*, when we had dined on the canopy, used as a table, above the engine whilst the engine throbbed to a flow of TVO (tractor vaporising oil)!

I was miserable! At least, it was snug below. I had little interest in the proceedings. Then the forward movement stopped.

What had happened? Jim had decided he had reached a spot where there were signs of fish. I ventured into the wheelhouse. Sumburgh lay to the west. On the sea, the fishing-fleet from Shetland was dotted about. Radios crackled. None of the skippers were giving away info to rival crews.

These waters which are readily storm-tossed, stretched calmly to the horizon. The light blue of the late evening summer sky was reflected in the stillness of the sea. With good sea-legs I should have appreciated it all. But, it was cool. Air temperatures above the North Sea are seldom warm. I went below.

The calm above did not reign here. The sturdy drifters that can plough their way home in a storm, are built for wallowing. The *Venture* wallowed, as if relaxing from days and nights of pounding from earlier trips.

Mine was a fitful night of catnaps and bouts with the bucket! The herring could slither into the fish-hold as the nets came aboard in the dawn. 'Just let's get back to Lerwick', was my main thought.

The catch was aboard. We turned about. We had a good load of fish. It was a blessing in more ways than one. The weight of the herring improved the *Venture*'s stability. I bucked up and almost began to enjoy the experience.

It is one thing to gain one's sea-legs. It is another to lose them ashore.

Jim had disappeared with a sample of the catch. Fishing is only one side of the business. Selling is another. Quality ensures better prices. 'Bruck', smaller and damaged fish are only fit for the fish-meal plant at Heogan on Bressay.

We knew there was such a plant whenever the wind blew from a certain north-easterly angle. Fortunately for Lerwegians, the wind doesn't often blow in from that quarter! Nothing can seal out that stench. If it prevails at mealtimes, it is so nauseating, it puts folk off their food!

During Jim's absence, crew members were preparing to unload the catch. The winch coiled a rope hauling baskets of herring from the hold. The winchman had a knack of twisting the rope to haul away and releasing it when the load was on the quayside. The catch was measured in crans. There was keen competition to record the biggest catch of the season for which a trophy was presented at a celebratory evening.

Weariness was getting the better of me. I needed to be home and in bed. Suddenly, as I stepped ashore, the solid masonry of the quay began to rise and fall disturbingly. I was staggering like a drunk. Worse was to come. I had little time for greetings and recounting the adventure. 'Let me get to bed!' was all I could think. In the bathroom, everything began to sway, ceiling, floor, walls, mirror. I felt as if I'd stepped into some crazy side-show in a fairground. It was only when sleep overcame me that things settled into place. I ought to have learnt my lesson. A second trip would have to be undertaken. I had failed to carry out my intention of filming this important facet of Shetland life. I had taken a few shots of the sail down the coast and the evening sight of the fleet bobbing in the water. I still had to film the hauling in of the nets.

The chance came later. This time the *Venture* headed out of the North Mooth, bound for Muckle Flugga, the northernmost outcrop of the archipelago.

It is aptly named. It marks the presence of the 'big bird-island', as I was to discover.

This trip was far less attractive. We were off in roughish weather. The bows rose quite considerably to dip equally alarmingly next moment. Thinking to take my mind off the movement of the boat, Jim gave me a shot at the wheel. In some ways, that made matters worse, as I was more aware of the rise and fall of the bows, trying to keep a line on a distant mark. Yet, despite all the discomfort, the torture was worthwhile.

Next morning, my camera was whirring at about 5 o'clock. The nets were being hauled aboard against the orange and fiery red streaks of the early day on a cloudless sky backdrop. Joe, his partners and the rest of the crew, were hauling in the drift-nets, which had been hanging like lethal curtains of mesh in the path of the shoals.

Herring were caught in the nylon squares, some less securely than others, for they fell back into the sea. Their new-found freedom was short-lived. Like Stukas over Dunkirk, Gannets were diving, wings folded, so that they were for all the world just powerful feathered darts, unerringly aimed at the target, their breakfast!

They seemed unaware of the boat and men, so intent they were on their meal. The net hung over the side, just feet away. The air above was filled with a screeching whirl of hungry birds. Watchful, beyond the mêlée, the Bonxies were holding themselves ready to harry a fish-laden Gull. The Arctic Skuas are masters of flight, wheeling and diving on the purveyor of their meal. It is as if, in some fastidious way, they do not mean to get their wings wet at the breakfast-table.

Later, back on shore, I calculated what the film had cost me in time and torment. For a mere five minutes of documentary, I had subjected myself to something like forty hours at sea, of which only three or four had anything pleasurable about them! Now, I cannot estimate the delight of recalling those hours and the friendship that stemmed from them.

FAREWELL!

OUR STAY in Shetland was to come to an end. In those later days, we were making decisions. On the one hand was the prospect of owning a home in Lerwick. Whilst we were pursuing this line, a post of comparable responsibility to my head of department position, was on offer at Forfar Academy in the county of Angus.

We knew fine, that two people would be only too delighted to have us back in the area. My in-laws were no longer quite so able. They had been a great help to us as we settled down in married life. In return, they had relied on their daughter's help and company. It had been only a tuppenny phone call away then and a few minutes' drive in a car. Our stay in Shetland had altered all that.

We also had to consider what permanent residence in the north land would mean. From a family point of view there would be every chance that we should lose them once their schooldays were over. Further education would necessarily take them to mainland Scotland or beyond. Perhaps, they would never return. Once they left, we should have no direct family contacts in the islands.

We made the decision. Whichever came first, the house or the job, we'd take it. The job won!

How can we say whether we won or lost? Family separation has been our lot. We are slightly better off in that we can reach some of the family directly (we could reach them on foot, if it came to a pinch!). But, the Canadian branch is proof of what we feared might happen. In Alberta, they are a long, long way away, and it means a flight. We have met but only rarely, and only slightly less than with the other two branches of the family. The south of England is more accessible. Still, it is not like going to Gran's was, when our bairns were little or when I was a lad!

We came home, in one sense, to quite a few of the Scottish members of the clan; but, we made a whole host of friends in the north. Contact is maintained by phone or letter. On occasion, we have met in Aberdeen. It has been a special privilege to entertain some of those dear friends in our home.

Our sojourn was a 'special time' as our eldest put it. She has managed back and introduced her husband to the charm of the folk and the country. She keeps in touch, too. My one regret is that I did not trace my own forebears. One came out of the Simmer Dim to marry a Geordie lass from Shields!

'ENVOI'

A POEM I wrote appeared in *The New Shetlander* under the title: 'Farewell to The Croft by Swining Voe'. My hope is that it makes a fitting end to my story.

For us, as a family, it embodies elements which we shall always associate with Shetland, its climate, its land and seascapes, but, most of all, its folk, their pace of living, their friendliness and also their respect for the wish of those who wanted to remain aloof.

FAREWELL TO THE CROFT BY SWINING VOE

The wind and the salt spray steam over the Isles.
Though still 'tis high Summer, gone are its smiles.
Green leaves are burnt brown and flowers droop dying.
To leeward the sea lies calmly a-sighing.

Above the thatched roof peat-reek swirls no more.
No noost holds the boat safe high on the shore.
Away it has borne to the head of the voe
Those kindly, good folk whose age was the foe.

Sheep to be herded, their wool gently roo-ed,
Wary, tread cliff-path to bring home shop food!
Short days of winter and oil-lamps to trim,
Burdensome chores as eyesight grows dim.

All this is past now; they're well settled in.
Their modern-style home greets both kith and kin.
The flick of a switch brings news, heat and light.
There's time to talk over years past, memories bright.

So Jeanie and Lawrie, long may you both share
These comforts together earned many a year.
Your door aye'll be open; we are sure of good cheer.
And long we shall crack of days past and friends dear.

The Shetland Islands

Muckle
Flugga

Herma
Ness Saxa
Vord

Baltasound

UNST

ATLANTIC
OCEAN

FETLAR

Mid
Yell Brough Lodge

YELL

Yell
Sound

Toft
Sullom
Voe
Scatsta
Mavis
Grind Dales Lunna
Voe The Croft
St Magnus
Bay Brae Swining
Voe
MUCKLE ROE Vidlin
Voe Laxo Symbister
Voe
PAPA **VEMENTRY** **WHALSAY**
STOUR **PAPA**
LITTLE

**OUT
SKERRIES**

Nesting

Isles of Gletness

Decca
Station

VAILA Weisdale

LERWICK **NOSS**
Scalloway Bressay
TRONDRA Gulberwick The Ward Sound
FOULA Hamnavoe Easter **BRESSAY**
Bridge End Quarff
Clift **BURRA**
Sound Wester
Quarff

HAVRA

Sand
Bigton Lodge **MOUSA**
St Ninian's
Isle

NORTH
SEA

Fitful
Head
Sumburgh
Bay of Jarlshof
Quendale

The Kames

Clift Hills

FAIR ISLE
(approx. 20 miles
south of Sumburgh)

— 71 —

GLOSSARY:

Ayre:	a sandy causeway linking an island to the main shore.
Breeks:	Scots form of breeches = trousers.
Dookin':	dooking, Scots for ducking, putting one's head under water.
Broch:	a Pictish clan dwelling and fort, built of stone slabs without mortar in a milk-bottle shape of concave sides.
Dry-stane:	Scots for dry stone.
Dyke:	Scots for a wall, usually linked with 'dry-stane', no mortar in its construction.
Fitful:	from Norwegian 'hvit' = white and 'ful', bird, perhaps a reference to a gull colony (plumage and guano!)
Flit:	Scots for to move house or to transport from one place to another.
Flit-boat:	used for transporting from a ship at anchor to the shore.
Flugga:	Bird Island, from Norse 'flug', a bird and the ending 'a' like 'ay', meaning island.
Foula:	another version of the above.
Furth of:	away from, out of a place.
Geo:	a narrow rocky inlet.
Geordie:	a native of Tyneside, N.E. England, but also more broadly embracing folk from the Tees to the Tweed.
Griddle:	Scots for a flat iron plate for baking cakes.
Lochan:	a small loch or tarn.
Mavis Grind:	the 'gate' to the north-west, marked as North Mavine on the map.
Muckle:	Scots for large, big or much.
Neesick:	Porpoise.
Peterhead:	fishing port on the Aberdeenshire coast, site of a penitentiary.
Piltock:	Shetland name for the coalfish or saithe.
Reek:	Scots for smoke. 'Auld Reekie' = Edinburgh.
Reestit:	Shetland for cured by drying or smoking.
Roup:	an auction.
Skarf:	Shetland for cormorant or shag.
Smoor:	damp down a fire so that it smoulders.
Sooth Mooth:	the southern entrance to Bressay Sound and Lerwick Harbour.
Sooth-moother:	a person coming from the Scottish mainland or beyond, somewhat derogatory, not a Shetlander.
Stour:	Norwegian for 'big'.
Tystie:	guillemot.
Voe:	bay or sea inlet.